Better Homes and Gardens®

A MERRY CHRISTMAS IN CROSS-STITCH

By Mimi Shimmin

Better Homes and Gardens® Books
Des Moines, Iowa

Better Homes and Gardens ® Books, an imprint of Meredith ® Books:
President, Book Group: Joseph J. Ward
Vice President, Editorial Director: Elizabeth P. Rice
Executive Editor: Maryanne Bannon
Senior Editor: Carol Spier
Associate Editor: Ruth Weadock
Copyeditor: Barbara Machtiger
Production Manager: Bill Rose

Better Homes and Gardens ® A MERRY CHRISTMAS IN CROSS-STITCH
was prepared and produced by Chapelle Ltd., P.O. Box 9242, Ogden, Utah 84409.
Owner: Jo Packham
Staff: Trice Boerens, Jennifer Burnette, Gaylene Byers, Holly Fuller, Cherie Hanson, Holly Hollingsworth, Susan Jorgensen, Lorin May, Jackie McCowen, Florence Stacey, Corinna Souder, Nancy Whitley, Lorrie Young
Photography: Ryne Hazen, Gary Rohman

ISBN: 0-696-20034-1 (hardcover)
ISBN: 0-696-20361-8 (softcover)
Library of Congress Catalog Card Number: 93–086663

Printed in the United States of America
10 9 8 7 6 5 4 3 2

All of us at Better Homes and Gardens ® Books are dedicated to offering you, our customer, the best books we can create. We are particularly concerned that all of our instructions for making projects are clear and accurate. Please address your correspondence to Customer Service, Meredith ® Press, 150 East 52nd Street, New York, NY 10022.

If you would like to order additional copies of any of our books, call 1-800-678-2803 or check with your local bookstore.

MERRY CHRISTMAS

Handmade decorations and gifts create

a special glow that is rekindled each new holiday season.

From the smallest hand-stitched hair bow to the most splendid,

glittering tree skirt, every cherished object recalls favorite times of

Christmases past. The bright, appealing cross-stitch projects in this book offer

varied delights to charm every taste. The love and caring that you

lavish upon these projects ensures that each one will bring

beauty and joy to holiday seasons yet to come.

For your convenience, all projects in this book
have been ranked according to
their recommended level of expertise.

★ = Novice

★★ = Intermediate

★★★ = Advanced

Look for the rankings next to the code for each project.

CONTENTS

VICTORIAN CHRISTMAS

For the Victorians, Christmas
was a special time.
Cherished friends and family
gathered for festive meals, games,
and gift-giving. Handmade gifts,
so treasured then, still say, "I care."
Express your old-fashioned
sentiment by stitching this
lovely trio of beaded rose designs–
a wreath, ornaments, and
a pretty sewing set.

VICTORIAN CHRISTMAS

WREATH

SAMPLE
Stitched on ivory Aida 14 over 1, the finished design size is 10 1/4" x 10 1/4". The fabric was cut 17" x 17". Because of the beadwork, the design can only be stitched on 14-count fabric. See Suppliers for Mill Hill Beads.

★★★ Anchor   DMC (used for sample)

Step 1: Cross-stitch (2 strands)

Anchor		DMC	
50	–	605	Cranberry-vy. lt.
66	✗	3688	Mauve-med.
42	◢	3350	Dusty Rose-dk.
44	∴	814	Garnet-dk.
897	▲	221	Shell Pink-vy. dk.
210	☐	562	Jade-med.
862	■	3362	Pine Green-dk.
381	△	938	Coffee Brown-ultra dk.
403	○	310	Black

Step 2: Mill Hill Beads

·	02018	Crystal Pink
☐	00553	Old Rose
✗	03003	Antique Cranberry
∴	00561	Ice Green

SEWING SET

SAMPLE
All three items are stitched on ivory Aida 14 over 1. The finished design size for the scissors case is 2 1/8" x 4 3/8". The fabric was cut 6" x 10". The finished design size for the pincushion is 4 7/8" x 4 7/8". The fabric was cut 9" x 9". The finished design size for the box lid is 5" x 5". The fabric was cut 9" x 9". Because of the beadwork, the designs can only be stitched on 14-count fabric. See Suppliers for Mill Hill Beads and wooden box.

Wreath, top left • Stitch Count: 143 x 143

SCISSORS CASE MATERIALS

- Completed cross-stitch; matching thread
- 3" x 6" piece of un-stitched ivory Aida 14.
- 3" x 6" piece of white cotton fabric
- 5" x 6" piece of fleece
- ½ yard of ¹⁄₁₆"-diameter black cording
- Black thread
- Beading needle
- 100 black seed beads
- One ³⁄₈"-diameter faceted black bead
- One ³⁄₁₆"-diameter faceted black bead

DIRECTIONS
All seams are ¼".

1. Trim completed design piece according to heavy black lines on graph. Using design piece as pattern, cut scissors case back from unstitched Aida 14 and two lining pieces from white fabric.

2. Cut fleece into two 2½" x 6" pieces. Center and baste one piece to case back and remaining piece to wrong side of design piece. With right sides together, stitch back and design piece, leaving top and one edge open. Turn. Slipstitch edge closed.

3. Stitch lining pieces together, leaving top and one edge open; do not turn. Slide lining over case, aligning tops and seams. Stitch around top. Turn through opening. Slipstitch opening closed. Tuck lining inside case.

4. Hand-sew cording to case, beginning on seam at top edge, continuing around case to opening, around opening, and finishing at starting point.

5. To make tassel, use black thread and beading needle to make 5 strands of 20 seed beads each. Pass thread ends through large faceted bead, then small faceted bead; knot. Attach tassel to bottom of case.

Wreath, top right

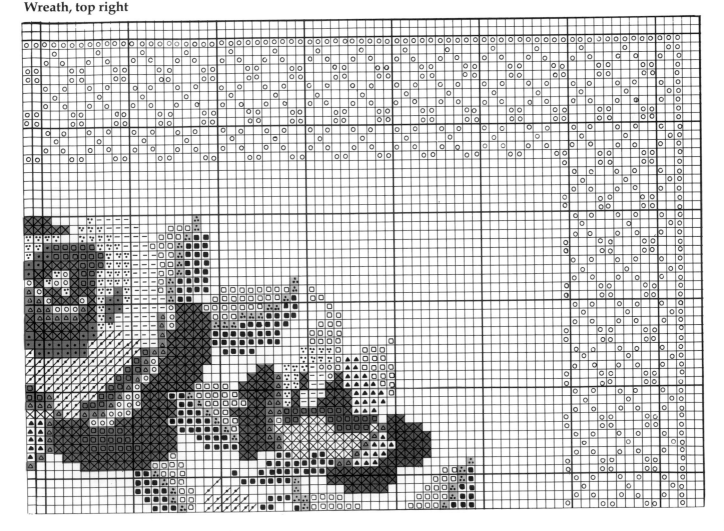

Wreath, bottom left

Wreath, bottom right

PINCUSHION MATERIALS

- Completed cross-stitch; matching thread
- 6" x 6" piece of un-stitched ivory Aida 14
- Polyester stuffing
- Heavy black thread
- Beading needle
- Three 500-count packages of black seed beads

DIRECTIONS

1. With design centered, trim completed design piece ½" from stitched latticework. Using design piece as pattern, cut pincushion back from unstitched Aida 14.

2. With right sides together, stitch design piece to back, rounding corners and leaving opening for stuffing. Turn. Stuff firmly. Slipstitch opening closed.

3. To make bead loops, use 20 beads per loop and make loops ⅜" wide. (See Beading Diagram above.) Begin on a corner and make 90 loops.

BOX LID MATERIALS

- Completed cross-stitch
- 5" x 5" piece of fleece
- 5" x 5" piece of card-board
- Spray adhesive
- Hot-glue gun and glue sticks
- Wooden box with lid (lid window should be 4½" x 4½")

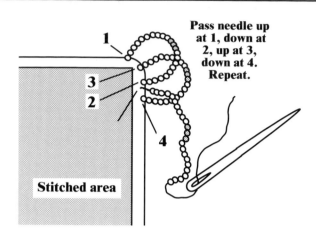

Pass needle up at 1, down at 2, up at 3, down at 4. Repeat.

1

3

2

4

Stitched area

Beading Diagram

DIRECTIONS

1. With design centered, trim completed design piece to 6¾" x 6¾".

2. Coat cardboard with spray adhesive. Press on fleece.

3. Center design piece over fleece. Wrap fabric edges snugly to back of cardboard, clipping corners as needed; hot-glue.

4. Insert design piece into box lid according to the manufacturer's instructions.

ORNAMENTS

SAMPLE
All three ornaments are stitched on ivory Aida 14 over 1. The finished design size for the medallion is 2¼" x 2¼". The fabric was cut 7¼" x 7¼". The finished design size for the 6-sided ornament is 1⅞" x 3⅜". The fabric was cut 9½" x 11". The finished design size for the diamond is 3⅛" x 3⅛". The fabric was cut 12" x 12". Because of the bead-work, the designs can only be stitched on 14-count fabric. See Suppliers for Mill Hill beads.

MATERIALS FOR ONE

- Completed cross-stitch ; matching thread
- 5" x 5" piece of un-stitched ivory Aida 14
- 5" x 10" piece of fleece
- Polyester stuffing
- Beading needle
- Heavy black thread
- Four 500-count packages of black seed beads

- One 5/16"-diameter faceted black bead
- 15" of ⅜"-wide picot-edged black ribbon

DIRECTIONS
All seams are ¼".

1. Trim completed medallion and 6-sided design pieces according to heavy black lines on graph. With design centered, trim diamond design piece to 4" x 4" . Using design piece as pattern, cut one orna-ment back from un-stitched Aida 14.

2. Cut fleece into two 5" x 5" pieces. Baste one piece to wrong side of design piece and remain-ing piece to ornament back. With right sides together, stitch design piece to ornament back, leaving one edge open for turning. Trim fleece from seam allowance. Turn. Stuff moderately. Slipstitch opening closed.

3. Sew one seed bead per line of fabric around seam or make ⅜"-wide bead loops, using 15 beads per loop. (See Beading Diagram above.) To make fringe, string 30 beads on thread, attach to bottom edge of orna-ment; repeat. To make tassel, make 5-7 strings of 20-30 beads each, pass-ing thread ends up through faceted bead. Add three more beads to top; attach tassel to bot-tom of ornament.

4. To make hanger, cut one 3" length and one 12" length from ribbon. Make bow with 12" length; notch ends. Tack bow to seam at top of ornament. Make loop with 3" length. With ends turned under and overlapping, tack loop to ornament back behind knot of bow.

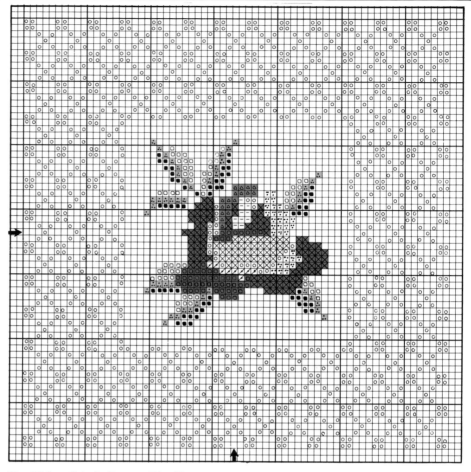

Box Lid • Stitch Count : 67 x 67

Box Lid, Pincushion ★★★

Anchor		DMC (used for sample)	
		Step 1: Cross-stitch (2 strands)	
50	−	605	Cranberry-vy. lt.
66	✕	3688	Mauve-med.
42	✐	3350	Dusty Rose-dk.
44	∴	814	Garnet-dk.
897	▲	221	Shell Pink-vy. dk.
210	□	562	Jade-med.
862	■	3362	Pine Green-dk.
381	◭	938	Coffee Brown-ultra dk.
403	○	310	Black
		Step 2: Mill Hill Beads	
	◆	02018	Crystal Pink
	▣	00553	Old Rose
	✕	03003	Antique Cranberry
	∴	00561	Ice Green

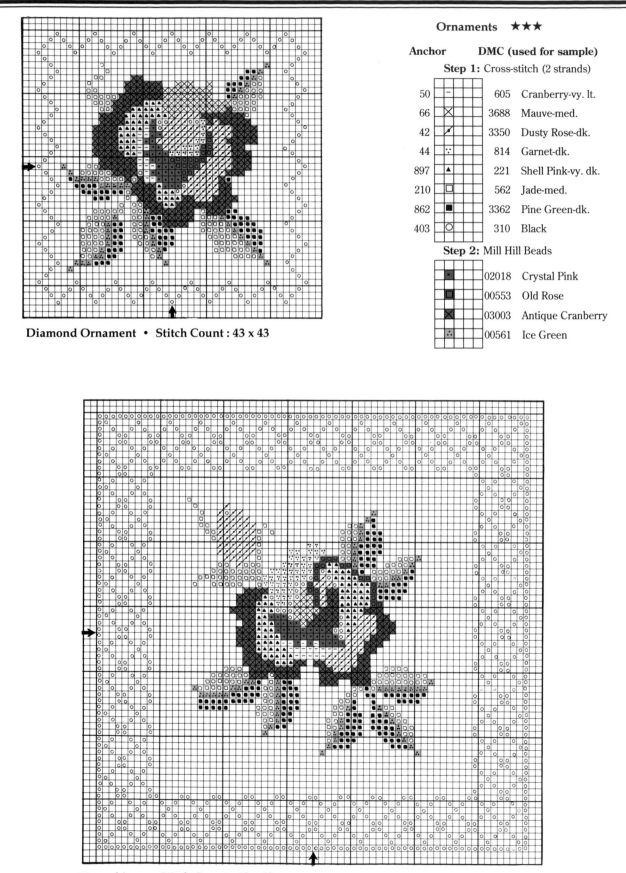

Ornaments ★★★

Anchor		DMC (used for sample)	
		Step 1: Cross-stitch (2 strands)	
50	−	605	Cranberry-vy. lt.
66	⊠	3688	Mauve-med.
42	⁄	3350	Dusty Rose-dk.
44	∷	814	Garnet-dk.
897	▲	221	Shell Pink-vy. dk.
210	□	562	Jade-med.
862	■	3362	Pine Green-dk.
403	○	310	Black

Step 2: Mill Hill Beads

02018	Crystal Pink
00553	Old Rose
03003	Antique Cranberry
00561	Ice Green

Diamond Ornament • Stitch Count : 43 x 43

Pincushion • Stitch Count : 68 x 68

14

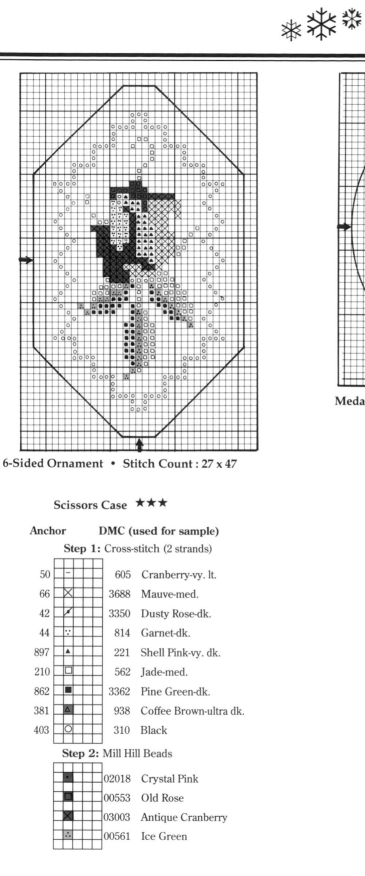

6-Sided Ornament • Stitch Count : 27 x 47

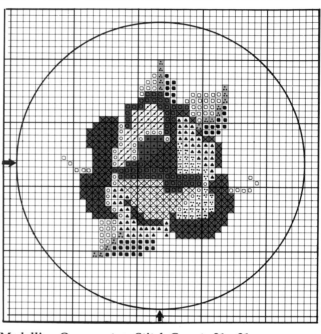

Medallion Ornament • Stitch Count : 31 x 31

Scissors Case ★★★

Anchor		DMC (used for sample)	
Step 1: Cross-stitch (2 strands)			
50	–	605	Cranberry-vy. lt.
66	✕	3688	Mauve-med.
42	◢	3350	Dusty Rose-dk.
44	⠢	814	Garnet-dk.
897	▲	221	Shell Pink-vy. dk.
210	☐	562	Jade-med.
862	■	3362	Pine Green-dk.
381	◬	938	Coffee Brown-ultra dk.
403	○	310	Black
Step 2: Mill Hill Beads			
	⦁	02018	Crystal Pink
	◨	00553	Old Rose
	✕	03003	Antique Cranberry
	⠋	00561	Ice Green

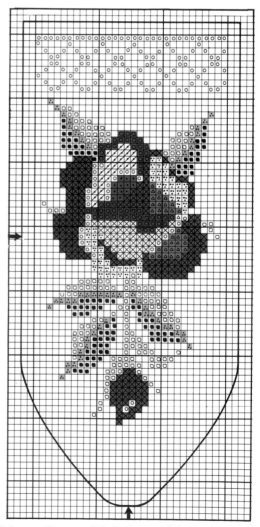

Scissors Case • Stitch Count : 30 x 61

NUTCRACKER CHRISTMAS

The charming tale of little Clara
and her Christmas dream is
a holiday classic. Stitch Clara,
the Nutcracker, the Wooden Soldier,
the Mouse King, and the rest
around this colorful tree skirt
and let them sparkle on your tree
as ornaments. You may conjure
a little Christmas magic of your own!

TREE SKIRT

SAMPLE

Stitched on white Country Aida 7 over 1, the finished design size is 27" x 27" for the ¼ of the design shown on the graph. Heavy black lines indicate repeats. The fabric was cut 62" x 62" for the complete tree skirt. The Wooden Soldier, Russian Dancer, Snow Queen, Sugar Plum Fairy, Chinese Girl and Nutcracker ornaments on pages 24-27 are also stitched on the tree skirt (see Placement Diagram).

(For ¼ of Design)

FABRICS	DESIGN SIZES
Aida 11	17⅛" x 17⅛"
Aida 14	13½" x 13½
Aida 18	11¾" x 11¾"
Hardanger 22	10½" x 10½"

MATERIALS

- Completed cross-stitch; matching thread
- Dressmaker's pen
- 3 yards of white fabric
- ½ yard of red fabric; matching thread.

DIRECTIONS

All seams are ¼".

1. Trim completed design piece to size and shape shown on Placement Diagram. Mark slash/opening with line of basting.

2. Cut and piece white fabric lining to 62" square. Place right side up on flat surface.

3. Center design piece wrong side up over lining; baste together. Trim excess lining. Stitch pieces together around marked opening only. Slash, remove all basting, and turn right side out.

4. From red fabric, cut 3"-wide bias strips, piecing as needed to make 6 yards of binding. Press ½" on long edges to wrong side of binding.

5. Fold and pin binding in half lengthwise over raw edge of tree skirt: Begin and end at slash, mitering corners and finishing ends neatly. Slipstitch in place.

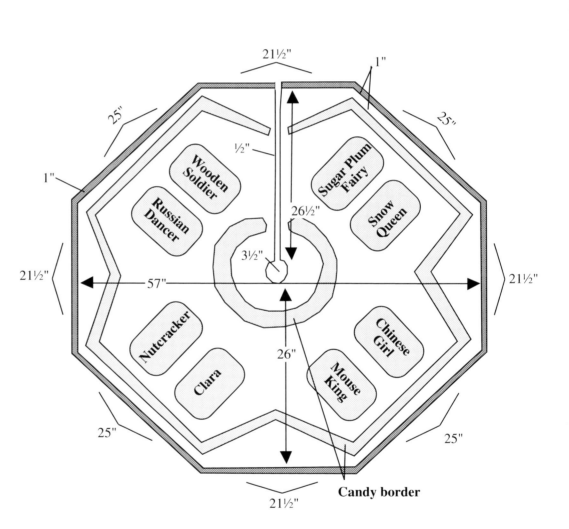

Tree Skirt Placement Diagram

Tree Skirt ★★

Anchor   **DMC (used for sample)**

Step 1: Cross-stitch (2 strands/tree skirt,
1 strand/ornaments)

Anchor			DMC	Color
1	·	⁄		White
290	·	⁄	973	Canary-bright
890	U	⌐	729	Old Gold-med.
307	+	⁄	783	Christmas Gold
304	■	⁄	741	Tangerine-med.
330	▣	⁄	947	Burnt Orange
49	−	⁄	963	Wild Rose-vy. lt.
24	○	⁄	776	Pink-med.
27	□	⁄	899	Rose-med.
46	△	⁄	666	Christmas Red-bright
86	▪	⁄	3608	Plum-vy. lt.
87	▲	⁄	3607	Plum-lt.
89	✕	⁄	917	Plum-med.
44	⁙	⁄	814	Garnet-dk.
119	▲	⁄	3746	Blue Violet-dk.
158	✕	⁄	775	Baby Blue-vy. lt.
128	I	⁄	800	Delft-pale
130	○	⁄	799	Delft-med.
133	∴	⁄	796	Royal Blue-dk.
255	+	⁄	907	Parrot Green-lt.
258	○	⁄	905	Parrot Green-dk.
229	✕	⁄	909	Emerald Green-vy. dk.
188	−	⁄	943	Aquamarine-med.
381	+	⁄	838	Beige Brown-vy. dk.
400	◤	⁄	317	Pewter Gray
403	∴	⁄	310	Black
	▽	⁄	001	Silver Balger #8 braid (tree skirt)
	▽	⁄		DMC Fil Argent Clair (ornaments)
	●	⁄	002	Gold Balger #8 braid (tree skirt)
	●	⁄		DMC Fil Or Clair (ornaments)

Step 2: Backstitch (2 strands/tree skirt,
1 strand/ornaments)

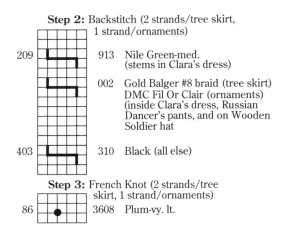

Anchor		DMC	Color
209		913	Nile Green-med. (stems in Clara's dress)
		002	Gold Balger #8 braid (tree skirt) DMC Fil Or Clair (ornaments) (inside Clara's dress, Russian Dancer's pants, and on Wooden Soldier hat
403		310	Black (all else)

Step 3: French Knot (2 strands/tree skirt, 1 strand/ornaments)

Anchor		DMC	Color
86	●	3608	Plum-vy. lt.

Tree skirt, top left

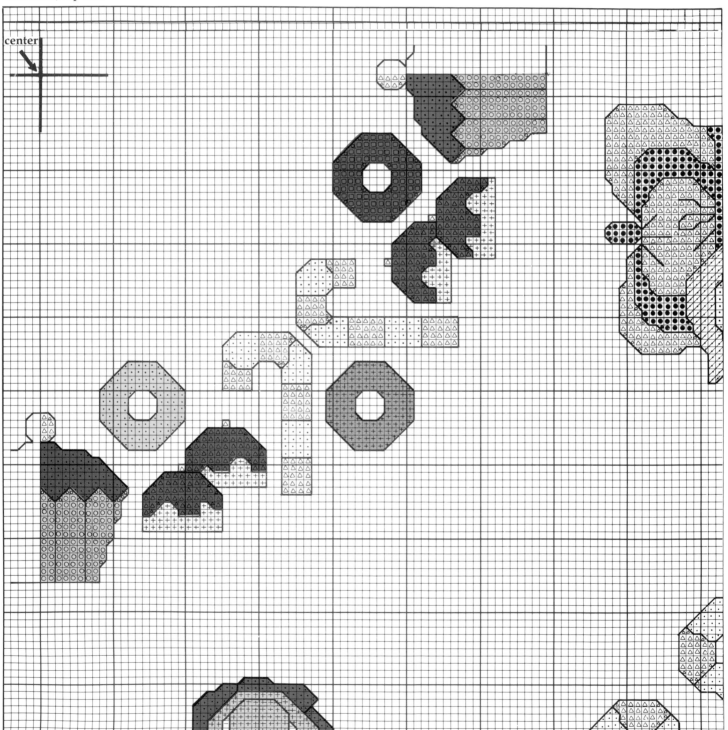

center

Tree skirt, top right

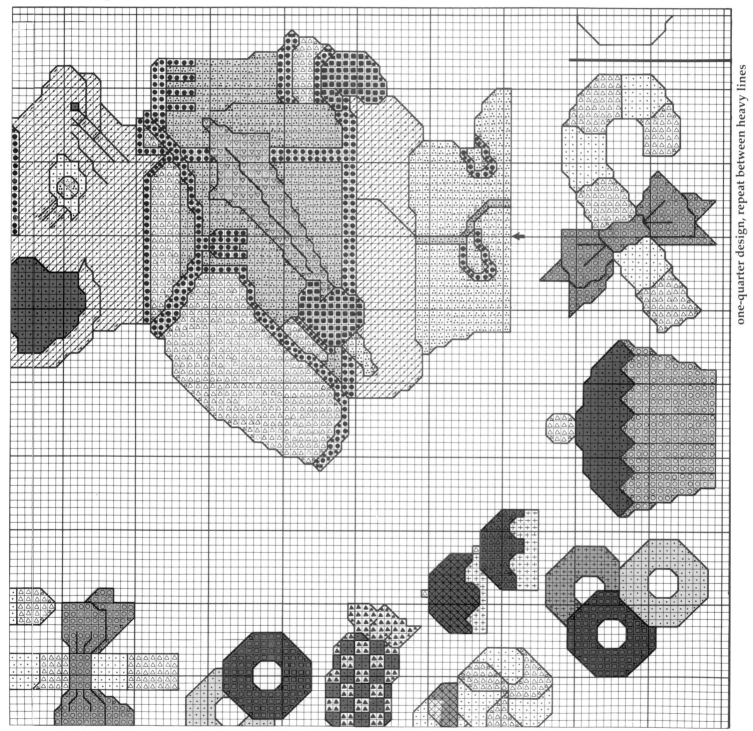

one-quarter design, repeat between heavy lines

Tree Skirt, bottom left

one-quarter design, repeat between heavy lines

Tree skirt, bottom right

ORNAMENTS

SAMPLE

All ornaments are stitched on white Perforated Plastic 14 over 1. The finished design sizes are: 2¼" x 6¼" for Wooden Soldier, 4½" x 4¾" for Russian Dancer, 3⅛" x 6⅜" for Snow Queen, 3⅛" x 6¼" for Sugar Plum Fairy, 2¾" x 6⅛" for Chinese Girl and 2⅞" x 6¼" for Nutcracker. The plastic was cut 9" x 11" for each. See Suppliers for Perforated Plastic and specialty thread.

(Wooden Soldier)
FABRICS	DESIGN SIZES
Aida 11	3" x 8"
Aida 18	1¾" x 4⅞"
Hardanger 22	1½" x 4"

(Russian Dancer)
FABRICS	DESIGN SIZES
Aida 11	5⅝" x 6⅛"
Aida 18	3½" x 3¾"
Hardanger 22	2⅞" x 3"

(Snow Queen)
FABRICS	DESIGN SIZES
Aida 11	4" x 8⅛"
Aida 18	2⅜" x 5"
Hardanger 22	2" x 4"

(Sugar Plum Fairy)
FABRICS	DESIGN SIZES
Aida 11	4" x 8"
Aida 18	2⅜" x 4⅞"
Hardanger 22	2" x 4"

(Chinese Girl)
FABRICS	DESIGN SIZES
Aida 11	3½" x 7¾"
Aida 18	2⅛" x 4¾"
Hardanger 22	1¾" x 3⅞"

(Nutcracker)
FABRICS	DESIGN SIZES
Aida 11	3¾" x 8"
Aida 18	2¼" x 4⅞"
Hardanger 22	1⅞" x 4"

★★Anchor   **DMC (used for sample)**

Step 1: Cross-stitch (2 strands/tree skirt, 1 strand/ornaments)

Anchor			DMC	
1				White
290			973	Canary-bright
890	U		729	Old Gold-med.
307	+		783	Christmas Gold
304	■		741	Tangerine-med.
330	▣		947	Burnt Orange
49	–		963	Wild Rose-vy. lt.
24	○		776	Pink-med.
27	□		899	Rose-med.
46	△		666	Christmas Red-bright
86			3608	Plum-vy. lt.
87	▲		3607	Plum-lt.
89	✕		917	Plum-med.
44			814	Garnet-dk.
119	▲		3746	Blue Violet-dk.
158	✕		775	Baby Blue-vy. lt.
128	I		800	Delft-pale
130	○		799	Delft-med.
133			796	Royal Blue-dk.
255	+		907	Parrot Green-lt.
258	○		905	Parrot Green-dk.
229	✕		909	Emerald Green-vy. dk.
188	–		943	Aquamarine-med.
381	+		838	Beige Brown-vy. dk.
400			317	Pewter Gray
403			310	Black
	▽		001	Silver Balger #8 braid (tree skirt)
				DMC Fil Argent Clair (ornaments)
	▽		002	Gold Balger #8 braid (tree skirt)
	●			DMC Fil Or Clair (ornaments)

Step 2: Backstitch (2 strands/tree skirt, 1 strand/ornaments)

Anchor		DMC	
209		913	Nile Green-med. (stems in Clara's dress)
		002	Gold Balger #8 braid (tree skirt) DMC Fil Or Clair (ornaments) (inside Clara's dress, Russian Dancer's pants, and on Wooden Soldier hat)
403		310	Black (all else)

Step 3: French Knot (2 strands/tree skirt, 1 strand/ornaments)

Anchor		DMC	
86	●	3608	Plum-vy. lt.

MATERIALS FOR ONE

- Completed cross-stitch
- Colored felt 1" larger all around than design
- Spray adhesive
- Pinking shears
- 9" length of thin gold cord
- Embroidery needle

DIRECTIONS

1. Trim edges of completed design piece one hole from stitched area.

2. Coat back of design piece with spray adhesive. Press on felt.

3. Using pinking shears and staying ¼" outside design, cut ornament shape from felt.

4. To make hanger, thread needle with gold cord (see Diagram 1). Insert needle through ornament near top edge, pulling cord halfway through. Insert cord ends through loop and tighten (see Diagram 2). Remove needle. Knot cord ends.

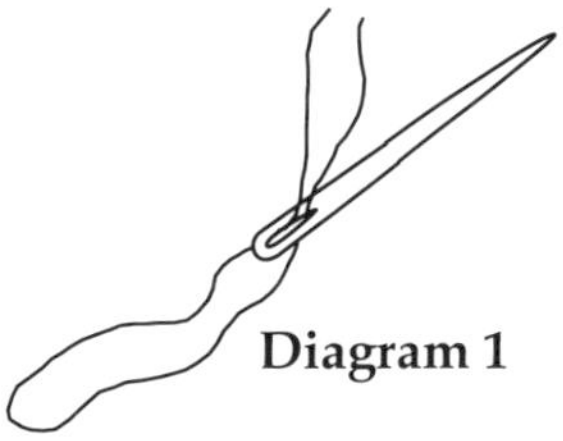

Diagram 1

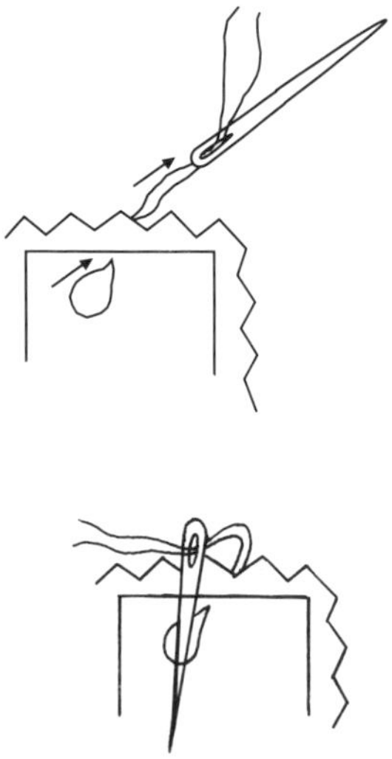

Diagram 2

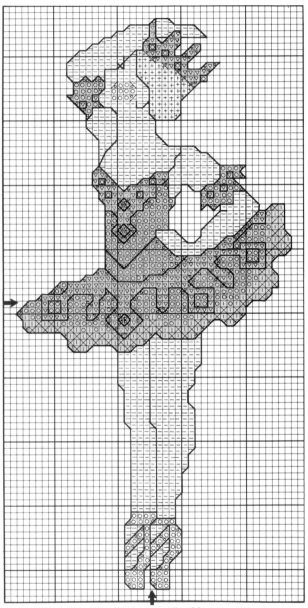

Nutcracker • Stitch Count: 41 x 88

Snow Queen • Stitch Count: 43 x 89

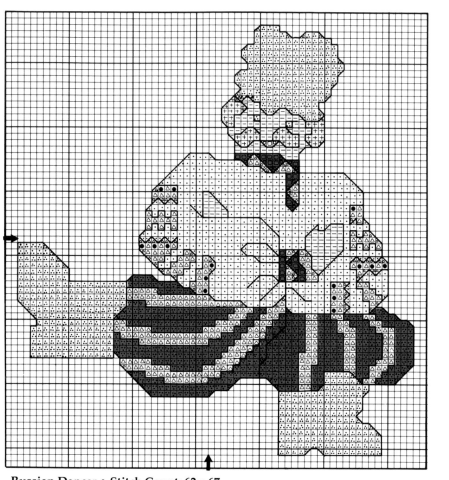

Russian Dancer • Stitch Count: 62 x 67

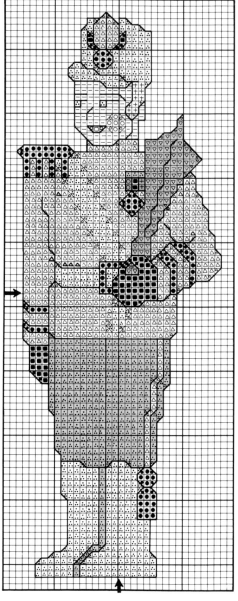

Wooden Soldier • Stitch Count: 32 x 88

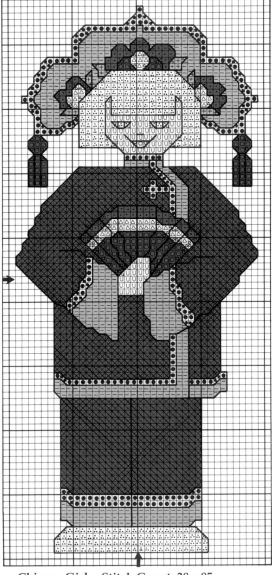

Chinese Girl • Stitch Count: 38 x 85

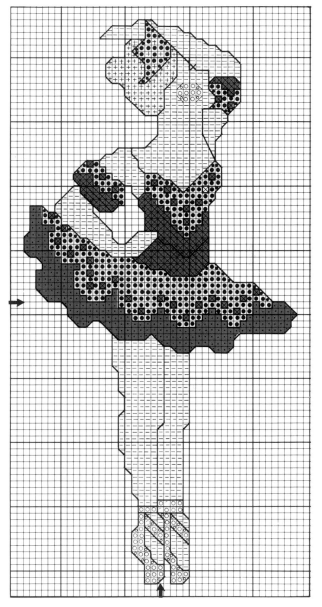

Sugar Plum Fairy • Stitch Count: 43 x 88

STAINED~ GLASS CHRISTMAS

Stained glass glows and shimmers with the special light of this special time of year. Capture its luminous colors in the beautiful and intricate patterns of a framed mirror, ornaments, and an elegant stocking– all set against dramatic black.

FRAMED MIRROR

SAMPLE
Stitched on black Aida 18 over 1, the finished design size is 11⅛" x 11⅛". The fabric was cut 18" x 18". The graph shows the lower left corner of the design; heavy black lines indicate repeats. See the Placement Diagram to complete the stitching.

FABRICS	DESIGN SIZES
Aida 11	18¼" x 18¼"
Aida 14	14⅜" x 14⅜"
Hardanger 22	9⅛" x 9⅛"

MATERIALS

- Completed cross-stitch
- 12½" x 12½" piece of mat board
- Craft knife
- Hot-glue gun and glue sticks
- Picture frame to fit mat board
- 8" x 8" mirror
- Shipping tape
- Finishing nails
- Brown wrapping paper to fit frame
- White glue
- Spray bottle with water

DIRECTIONS

1. With design centered, trim completed design piece to 14" x 14". Clip unstitched fabric in center of design piece (see Diagram 1).

2. Find center of mat board. Mark and cut out 5" x 5" opening (see Diagram 2).

3. Center design piece on mat board. Fold unstitched fabric in center through opening to back of mat board, leaving ⅛" of fabric showing on front (see photo). Secure on back with hot glue.

4. Keeping edges and stitching straight, fold remaining excess fabric to back; hot-glue.

5. Place design piece face down. Center mirror face down over opening; tape in place.

6. Insert design piece into frame. Secure with finishing nails.

7. Coat frame back with white glue. Press on brown paper. Spray paper lightly with water. It will shrink as it dries, ensuring a snug fit.

Repeat border as desired to fill.

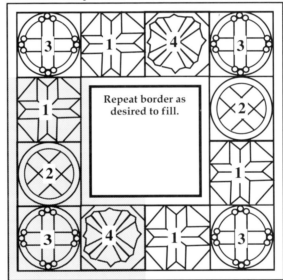

☐ = Area shown on graph

Placement Diagram

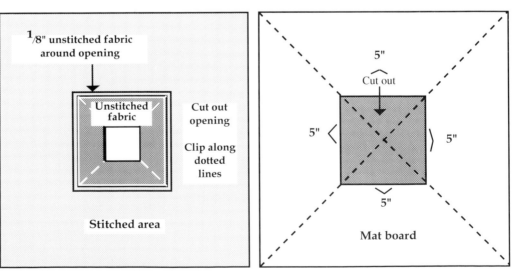

Diagram 1

Diagram 2

STOCKING

CUFF SAMPLE
Stitched on black Aida 14 over 1, the finished design size is 10¼" x 4⅛". The fabric was cut 30" x 10". The motifs on the cuff are taken from the Framed Mirror (see pages 34–35) and use the same code. Begin stitching in center of fabric.

FABRICS	DESIGN SIZES
Aida 11	13" x 5⅛"
Aida 18	8" x 3⅛"
Hardanger 22	6½" x 2⅝"

STOCKING MATERIALS

- Completed cross-stitch; matching thread
- Dressmaker's pen
- 1 yard of black moiré
- 2½ yards of ¼"-diameter black braided piping
- 7" of ⅜"-diameter black cording
- Two 4"-long black rayon tassels

DIRECTIONS
All seams are ¼".

1. Trim completed design piece to 20½" x 4¾". Using design piece as pattern, cut matching piece from black moiré for cuff lining.

2. From braided piping, cut two 20½" lengths. Stitch one length to right side of each long edge of design piece (see Diagram 1). With right sides together, stitch short ends of cuff; do not turn.

3. With right sides together, stitch short ends of cuff lining; turn right side out. Aligning seams, slide lining inside design piece. Stitch top edge of lining to design piece along stitching line of braided piping. Draw lining up out of design piece and down, so bottom edges align (see Diagram 2). Turn cuff; press with lining on inside.

4. To complete cuff, turn in raw edges of lining and cuff; slip-stitch in place.

5. To make hanger, loop ⅜"-diameter cording and baste ends, raw edges aligned, to cuff at seam.

6. Make stocking pattern on page 32. From black moiré, cut four stockings, reversing pattern for two.

7. Stitch braided piping to right side of one stocking piece. With right sides together, stitch stocking piece to one reversed stocking piece along stitching line of piping, leaving top open. Turn.

8. To make stocking lining, stitch remaining two stocking pieces with right sides together, leaving open at top and for 3" in seam above heel; do not turn. Slide lining over stocking, aligning top edges and seams.

Stitch around stocking top. Pull stocking through opening in lining, turning right side out. Slip-stitch opening closed. Tuck lining inside stocking.

9. Slide cuff over stocking so piping at top edge is ¼" above stocking top. Hand-sew cuff to stocking, securing hanger.

10. Attach tassels to hanger.

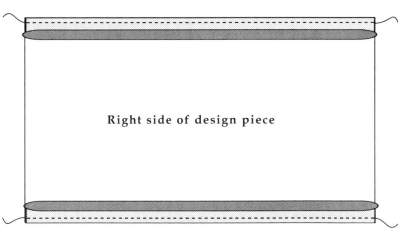

Right side of design piece

Diagram 1

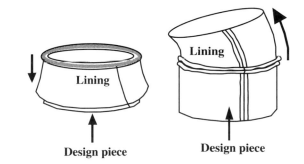

Lining

Design piece

Lining

Design piece

Diagram 2

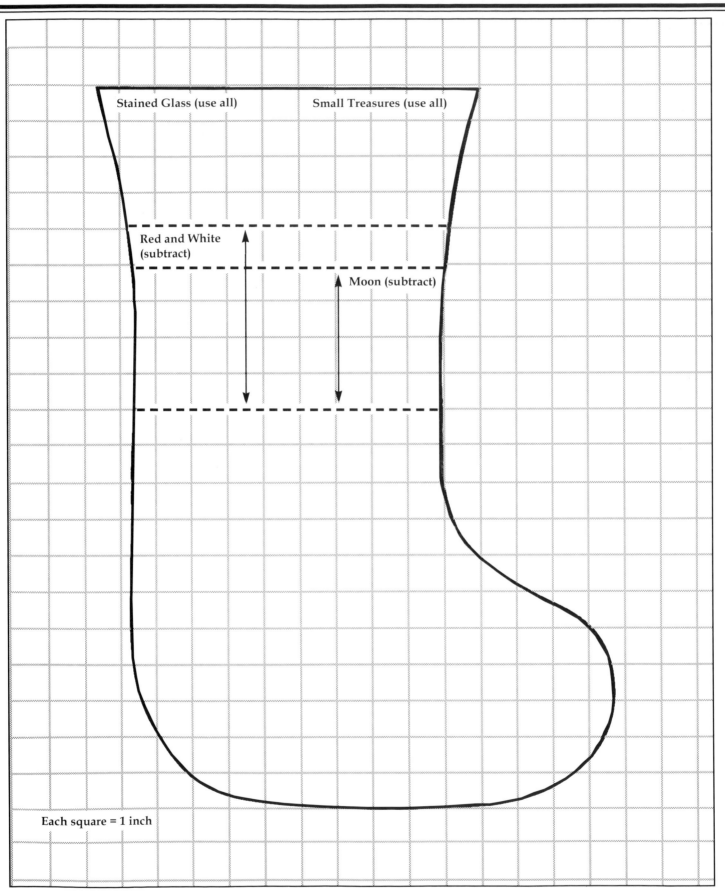

Stained Glass (use all)   Small Treasures (use all)

Red and White
(subtract)

Moon (subtract)

Each square = 1 inch

Stained Glass Stocking (also Moon Stocking, Red and White Stocking, Small Treasures Stocking) • Pattern

ORNAMENTS

SAMPLE
All four ornaments are stitched on black Aida 18 over 1. The finished design size for each is 3" x 3". The fabric for each was cut 8" x 8". The motifs are taken from the Framed Mirror and use the same code.

FABRICS	DESIGN SIZES
Aida 11	5" x 5"
Aida 14	3⅞" x 3⅞"
Hardanger 22	2½" x 2½"

MATERIALS FOR ONE

- Completed cross-stitch; matching thread
- 4" x 4" piece of un-stitched black Aida 18
- 4" x 8" piece of fleece
- Polyester stuffing
- 26" of ¹⁄₁₆"-diameter black cording

DIRECTIONS

1. Trim completed design piece all around ³⁄₈" from stitched area. Using design piece as pattern, cut ornament back from unstitched Aida 18.

2. Cut fleece into two 4" x 4" pieces. Center and baste one piece to wrong side of design piece and remaining piece to ornament back.

3. For hanger, cut a 2½" length from black cord-ing. Make loop and baste ends, raw edges aligned, to right side of design piece.

4. With right sides to-gether and edges align-ed, stitch design piece to ornament back, leav-ing one edge open for turning.

5. Trim seam allowance. Turn. Stuff moderately. Slipstitch opening closed.

6. Whipstitch remaining cording along seam of ornament, beginning and ending behind hanger.

Ornaments • Stitch Count: 55 x 55 for each

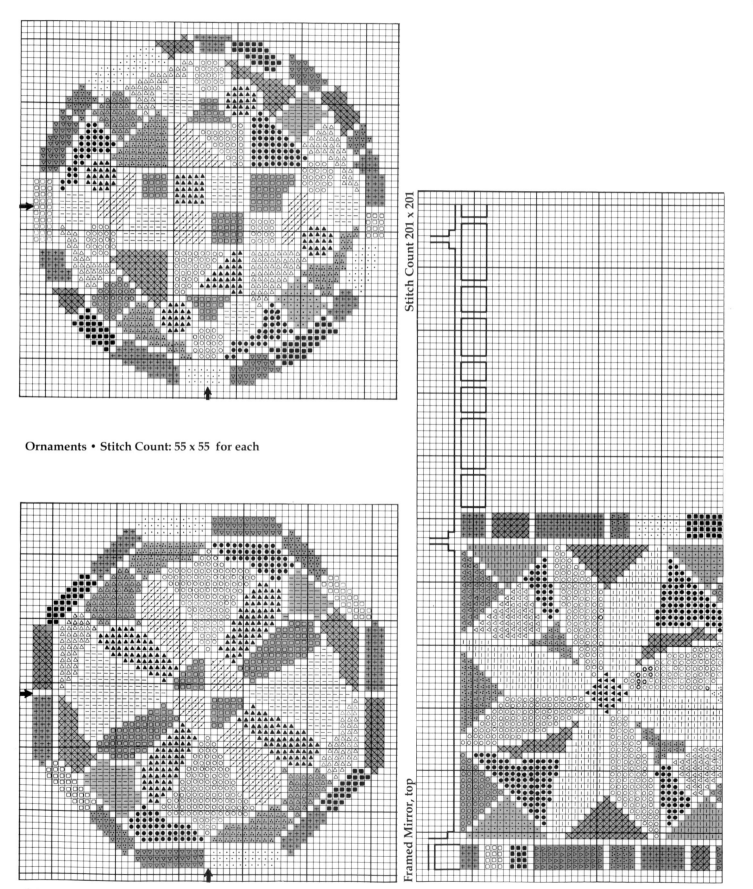

Ornaments • Stitch Count: 55 x 55 for each

Stitch Count 201 x 201

Framed Mirror, top

★★ **Anchor**   **DMC (used for sample)**

Step 1: Cross-stitch (2 strands)

298	–	972	Canary-deep
304	○	741	Tangerine-med.
308	▲	782	Topaz-med.
889	⁄	831	Olive Green-med.
330	▣	947	Burnt Orange
46	+	666	Christmas Red-bright
13	▽	347	Salmon-vy. dk.
20	⊠	498	Christmas Red-dk.
43	⸭	815	Garnet-med.
77	·	602	Cranberry-med.
87	☐	3607	Plum-lt.
89	■	917	Plum-med.
410	⸬	995	Electric Blue-dk.
145	△	334	Baby Blue-med.
131	●	798	Delft-dk.
164	⊠	824	Blue-vy. dk.
255	·	907	Parrot Green-lt.
258	○	905	Parrot Green-dk.
227	–	701	Christmas Green-lt.
229	△	909	Emerald Green-vy. dk.

Framed Mirror, bottom

THE TREE
OF LIFE

As the seasons change and
the new year approaches,
the Tree of Life remains
a timeless symbol of
renewal and hope.
This charming folk-art sampler
is a thoughtful complement
to a traditional Christmas tree.
The bold afghan makes
a gift of love and warmth.

AFGHAN

SAMPLE
Stitched on cream Gloria 14 Afghan Fabric over 2 , the finished design size for Block A (long sides) is 3½" x 28¼". The finished design size for Block B (corners) is 3½" x 3½". The finished design size for Block C (short sides) is 20" x 3½". One afghan fabric cut is 1.3 yards. See Afghan Diagram before beginning to stitch. See Suppliers for specialty fabric and thread.

Block A/Long Sides

FABRICS	DESIGN SIZES
Aida 11	2⅛" x 18"
Aida 18	1⅜" x 11"
Hardanger 22	1⅛" x 9"

Block B/Corners

FABRICS	DESIGN SIZES
Aida 11	2⅛" x 2⅛"
Aida 14	1¾" x 1¾"
Aida 18	1⅜" x 1⅜"
Hardanger 22	1⅛" x 1⅛"

Block C/Short Sides

FABRICS	DESIGN SIZES
Aida 11	12¾" x 2¼"
Aida 14	10" x 1¾"
Aida 18	7¾" x 1⅜"
Hardanger 22	6 ⅜" x 1⅛"

MATERIALS

• Completed cross-stitch

DIRECTIONS

1. To make fringe, measure 1⅝" from outside edge of design all around. Pull all horizontal threads outside measurement.

2. Count out 12 threads; knot. Repeat around afghan. Trim fringe to desired length.

SAMPLER

SAMPLE
Stitched on dirty linen Dublin Linen 25 over 2 threads, the finished design size is 11" x 14¾". The fabric was cut 17" x 21". See Suppliers for specialty thread.

FABRICS	DESIGN SIZES
Aida 11	12½" x 16⅞"
Aida 14	9¾" x 13¼"
Aida 18	7⅝" x 10¼"
Hardanger 22	6¼" x 8⅜"

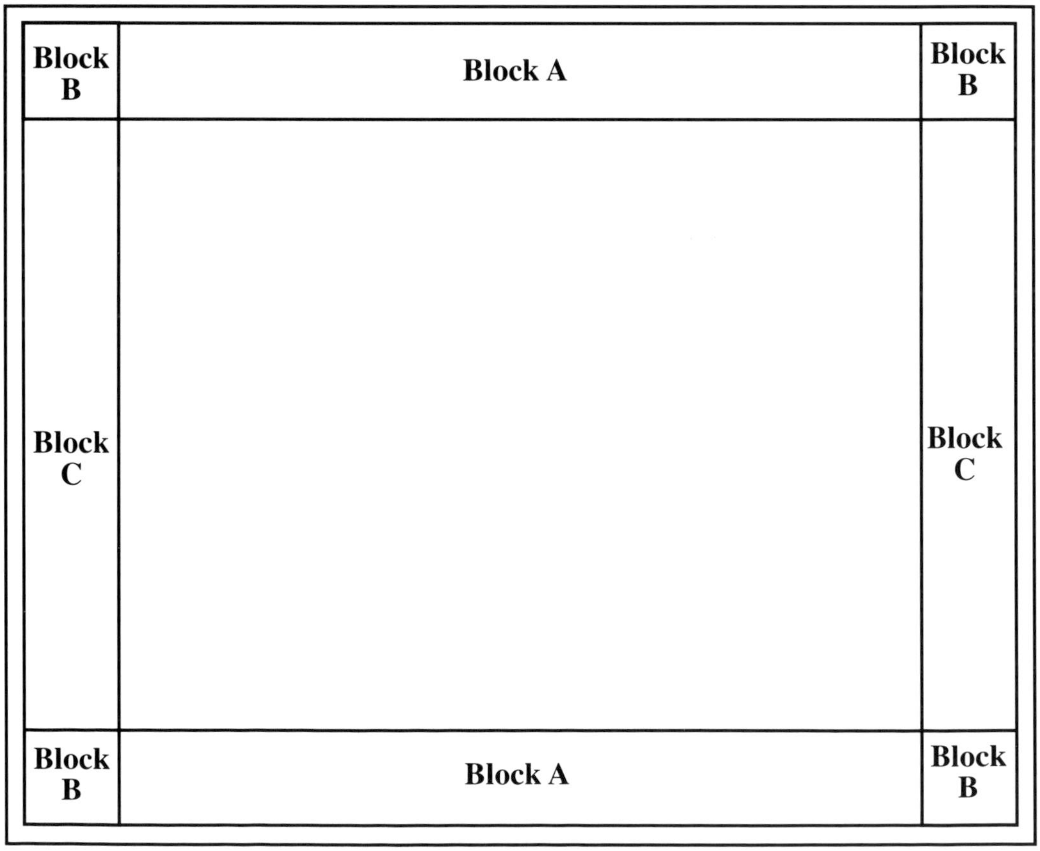

Block B	Block A	Block B
Block C		Block C
Block B	Block A	Block B

Afghan Diagram

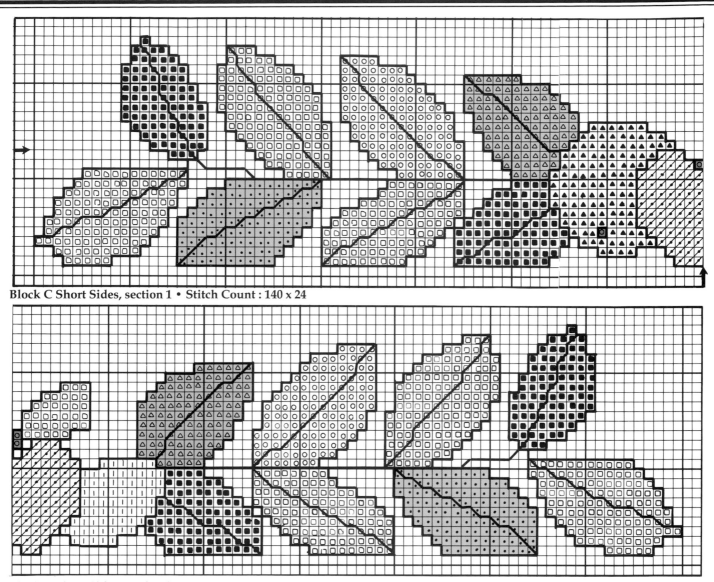

Block C Short Sides, section 1 • Stitch Count : 140 x 24

Block C Short Sides, section 2

Afghan ★

DMC Floss			DMC Medici (used for sample)	
Step 1: Cross-stitch (1 strand)				
725			8325	Topaz
947			8908	Burnt Orange
321			8126	Christmas Red
3777			8114	Terra Cotta-vy. dk.
3348			8419	Yellow Green-lt.
581			8401	Moss Green
580			8418	Moss Green-dk.
937			8417	Avocado Green-med.
367			8414	Pistachio Green-dk.
Step 2: Backstitch (1 strand)				
3371			8500	Black Brown

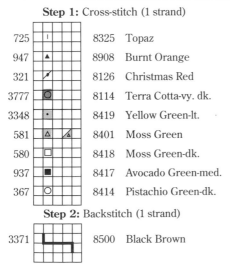

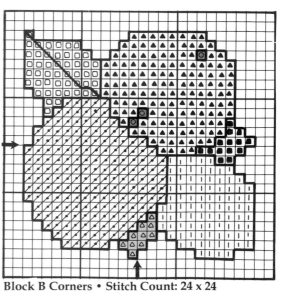

Block B Corners • Stitch Count: 24 x 24

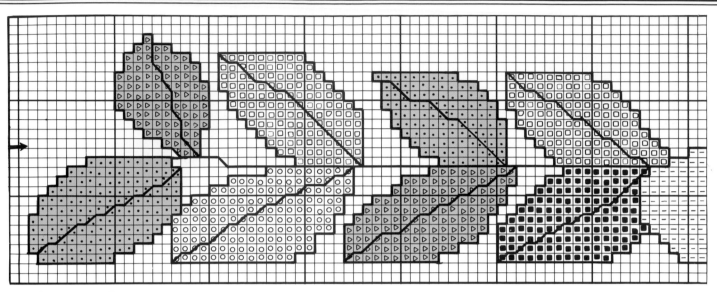

Block A Long Sides, section 1 • Stitch Count: 24 x 198

Sampler ★

DMC Floss   DMC Medici (used for sample)

Step 1: Cross-stitch (1 strand)

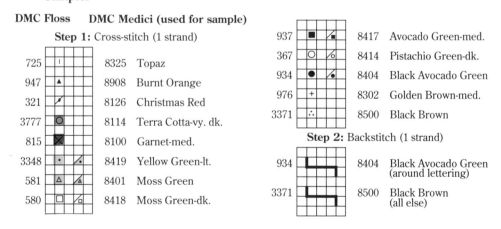

DMC Floss		DMC Medici	
725		8325	Topaz
947		8908	Burnt Orange
321		8126	Christmas Red
3777		8114	Terra Cotta-vy. dk.
815		8100	Garnet-med.
3348		8419	Yellow Green-lt.
581		8401	Moss Green
580		8418	Moss Green-dk.
937		8417	Avocado Green-med.
367		8414	Pistachio Green-dk.
934		8404	Black Avocado Green
976		8302	Golden Brown-med.
3371		8500	Black Brown

Step 2: Backstitch (1 strand)

934		8404	Black Avocado Green (around lettering)
3371		8500	Black Brown (all else)

Sampler, top left • Stitch Count: 137 x 185

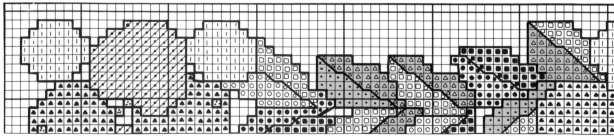

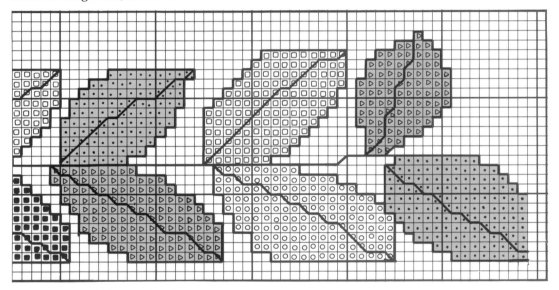

Block A Long Sides, section 2

Block A Long Sides, section 3

Sampler, top right

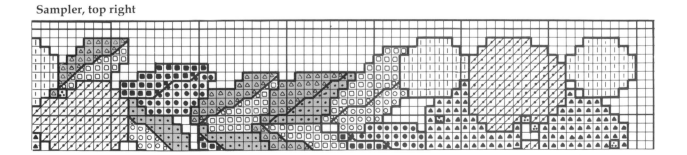

**Sampler,
center left**

Sampler,
center right

Sampler, bottom left

Sampler, bottom right

BLUE AND WHITE CHRISTMAS

The frosty, pale-blue of a clear winter sky, the crisp white of fresh snow–these are two of the colors of Christmas. Capture them both on a lavish stocking and three delicate ornaments. With the soft luster of faux pearls, white lace and ribbons, these designs will add a unique touch to your holiday decorations.

STOCKING

CUFF SAMPLE
Stitched on white Aida 14 over 1, the finished design size is determined by the letters stitched. The fabric was cut 17" x 7". If the name is too long to fit the matching stocking, stitch initials only.

CUFF MATERIALS

- Completed cross-stitch; matching thread
- 13½" x 3½" piece of white cotton fabric
- 27" of pearl piping
- ¾ yard of ½"-wide flat lace trim

DIRECTIONS
All seams are ¼ ".

1. With design centered, trim completed design piece to 13½" x 3½".

2. Cut pearl piping and lace trim in half. Pin one length of lace over one length of piping to right side of each long edge of design piece (see Diagram 1 on page 31). Position piping so top edge of lace is above it. Stitch. With right sides together, stitch short ends of cuff; do not turn.

3. With right sides together, stitch short ends of cotton fabric; turn right side out. Aligning seams, slide lining inside design piece.

Stitch Counts:
Fan: 75 x 41
Heart: 48 x 45
Butterfly: 61 x 55

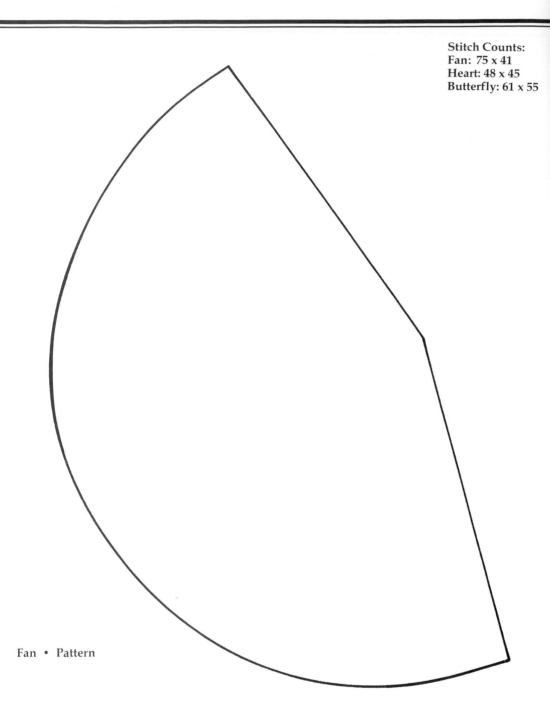

Fan • Pattern

Stitch top edge of lining to design piece along stitching line of piping and lace. Draw lining up out of design piece and down, so bottom edges align (see Diagram 2 on page 31). Turn cuff; press with lining on inside.

4. To complete cuff, turn in raw edges of lining and cuff; slipstitch in place. Set aside.

STOCKING SAMPLE
Stitched on delft blue Aida 14 over 1, the finished design size is 9⅜" x 10¼". The fabric was cut 13" x 18". Use white thread to attach pearls. Because of the beadwork, the design can only be stitched on a 14-count fabric. See Suppliers for specialty thread and pearls.

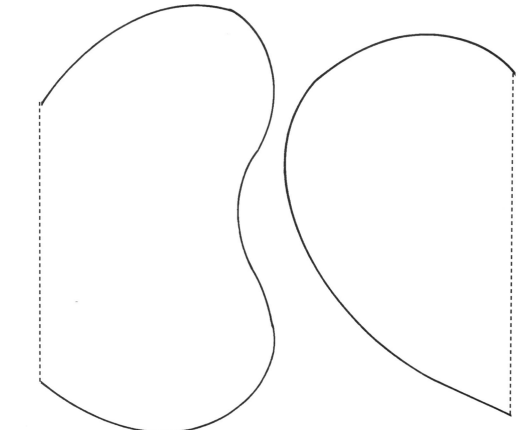

Butterfly, Heart Ornaments • Half Patterns

STOCKING MATERIALS

- Completed cross-stitch; matching thread
- 13" x 18" piece of un-stitched delft blue Aida 14
- ⅜ yard of blue cotton fabric
- 1 yard of ⅛" cotton cording
- ¼ yard of white satin
- Completed stocking cuff
- 44" of ⅜"-wide white, picot-edged ribbon
- 54" of ⅛"-wide white ribbon
- 30" of ⅛"-wide silver-centered, white ribbon
- 4" of ¼"-wide white, picot-edged ribbon
- 36" strand of craft pearls

DIRECTIONS

All seams are ½".

1. Make stocking pattern on page 52. With design horizontally centered and stocking top 3⅜" above top edge of stitched area, cut one stocking from design piece. Cut one stocking from unstitched Aida 14 for stocking back and two stockings from blue fabric for lining, reversing pattern as needed.

2. From white satin, cut 1¼"-wide bias strips, piecing as needed to equal 36". Cover cording to make piping.

3. Stitch piping to right side of design piece. With right sides together, stitch design piece to stocking back along stitching line of piping, leaving top open. Turn.

4. To make lining, stitch blue fabric stockings with right sides together, leaving open at top and for 3" in seam above heel; do not turn. Slide lining over stocking, aligning top edges and seams. Stitch around stocking top. Pull stocking through opening in lining, turning right side out. Slipstitch opening closed. Tuck lining inside stocking.

5. Slide cuff over stocking so pearl piping is above stocking top and name is centered on stocking front (see photo). Hand-sew cuff to stocking.

6. To make hanger, loop ¼"-wide ribbon and hand-sew ends to outside top edge of stocking cuff at heel seam.

7. To make ribbon and pearls bow, fold remaining ribbons into loops as desired with tails hanging free. Hand-sew to cuff over hanger ends. Gently tie craft pearls strand in a double bow, with ends hanging free. Hand-sew to center of ribbons. Trim ribbon tails as desired.

ORNAMENTS

SAMPLE

All three ornaments are stitched on delft blue Aida 14 over 1. The motifs are taken from the Stocking graph on pages 50–53 and use the same code. The finished design size for the fan is 5⅜" x 2⅞". The fabric was cut 10" x 8". Do not stitch the bow shown on the graph (see Step 3). The finished design size for the heart is 3⅜" x 3¼". The fabric was cut 8" x 8". The finished design size for the butterfly is 4⅜" x 3⅞". The fabric was cut 9" x 9". Because of the bead-work, the designs can only be stitched on 14-count fabric.

Materials For One

- Completed cross-stitch; matching thread
- 6" x 6" piece of un-stitched delft blue Aida 14
- Polyester stuffing
- ½ yard of ⅛"-wide or ⅜"-wide flat lace trim
- ⅛"-wide white, picot-edged ribbon and/or white ribbon with metallic silver center (see Step 3)

Directions

All seams are ¼".

1. Make pattern. Center completed design on pattern and cut out ornament shape. Also cut out ornament back from unstitched Aida 14.

2. Stitch lace trim to right side of design piece, scallops toward center and straight edge ⅛" from raw edge, and fol-lowing contours of shape. With right sides together, stitch design piece to ornament back along stitching line of trim, leaving an opening. Turn. Stuff moderately. Slipstitch opening closed.

3. Here are three ways to finish ornament. To make small bow, tie 8" length of ribbon into bow. Trim tails diagonal-ly. Tack knot to center top of ornament. To make hanger, loop 4" length of ribbon. Overlap ends and tack to ornament back. To make 5-looped bow, tie length of picot-edged ribbon into bow. Repeat with silver-centered rib-bon. Tack the bows together at knots. Loop 8" length of silver-cen-tered ribbon, leaving 3" tails. Trim tails diagonal-ly. Tack loop to knot of bows. Tack the complet-ed bow to front of orna-ment (see photo).

Stocking, top left • Stitch Count: 131 x 150

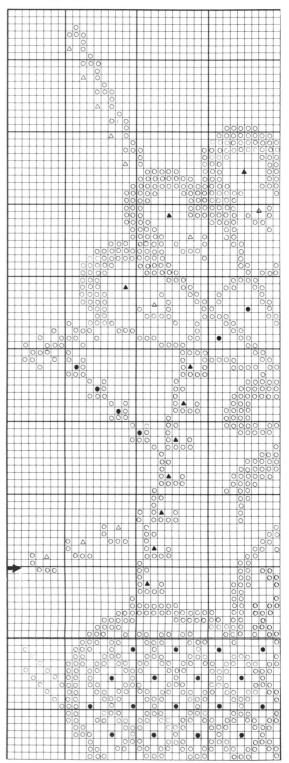

★★ DMC   Marlitt (used for sample)   Step 3: Beadwork

Step 1: Cross-stitch (2 strands)

White ◯ 800 White

Step 2: Backstitch (2 strands over 2 threads)

White └ 800 White

● 2.5mm pearl

▲ 3mm pearl

△ 3mm x 6mm pearl

Stocking, top right

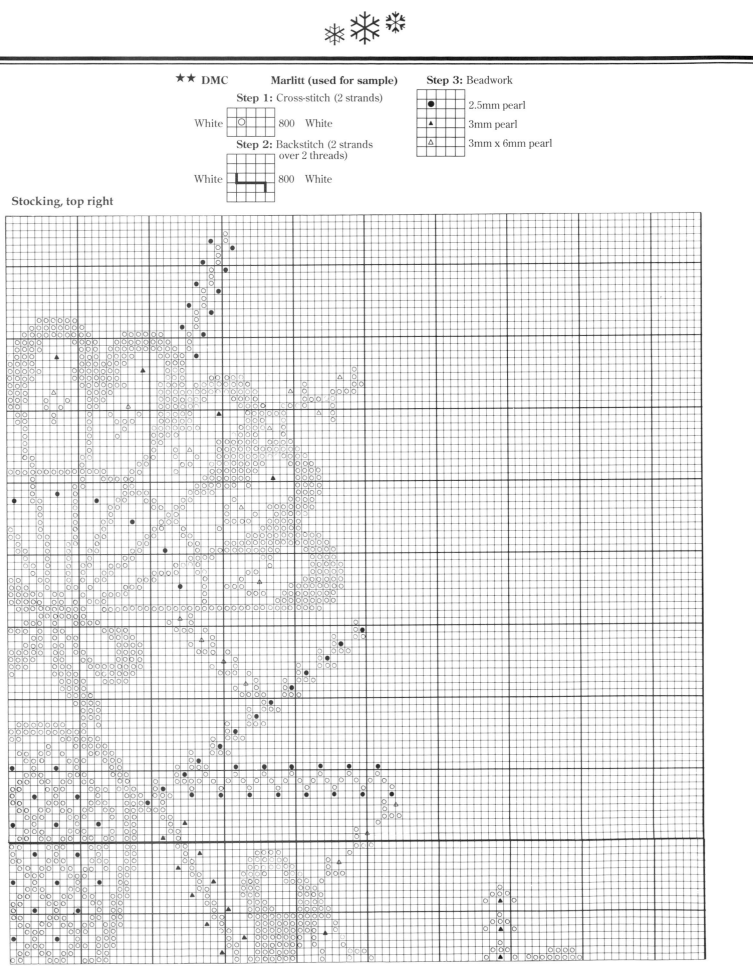

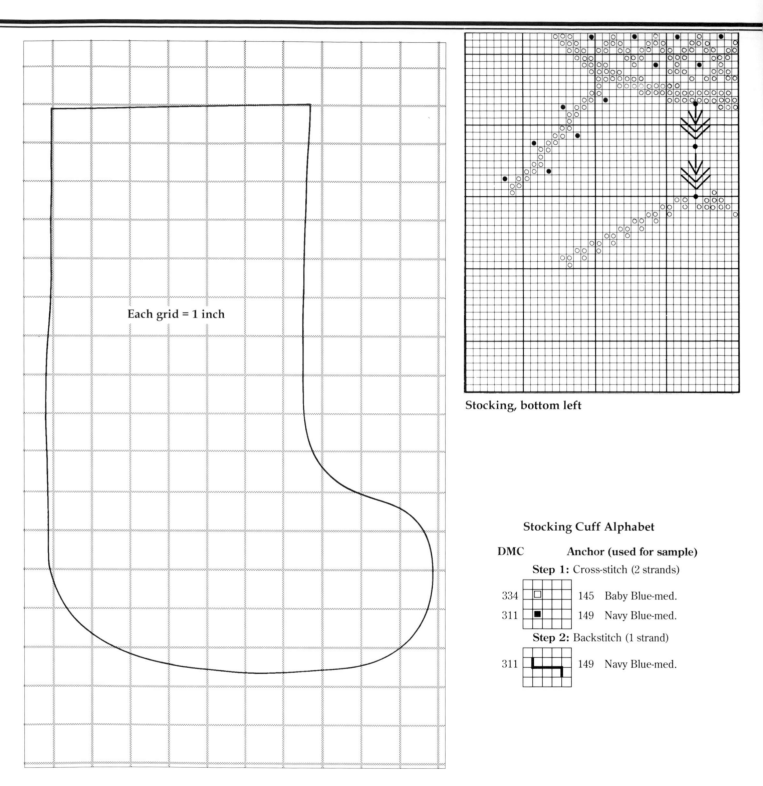

Each grid = 1 inch

Stocking, bottom left

Stocking Cuff Alphabet

DMC		Anchor (used for sample)
	Step 1: Cross-stitch (2 strands)	
334	☐	145 Baby Blue-med.
311	■	149 Navy Blue-med.
	Step 2: Backstitch (1 strand)	
311	⌐	149 Navy Blue-med.

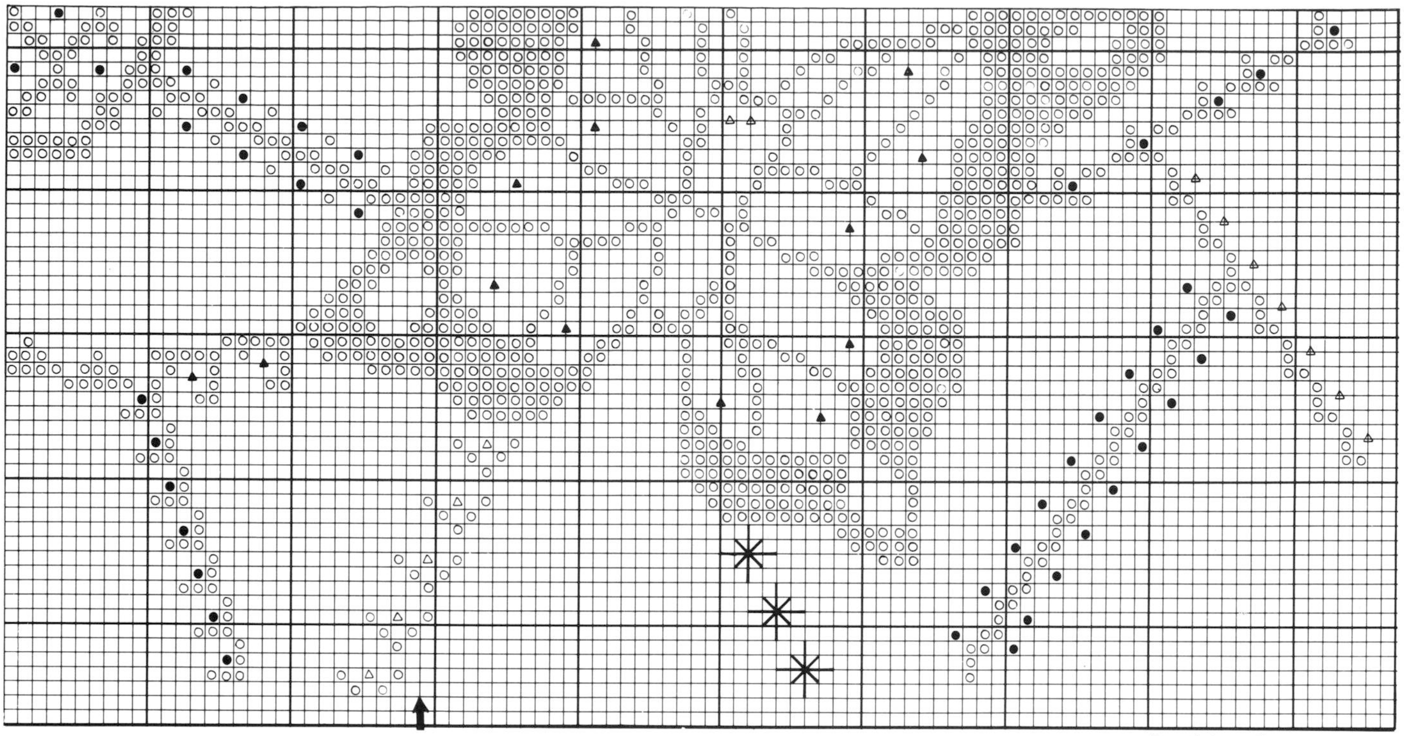

Stocking Cuff Alphabet

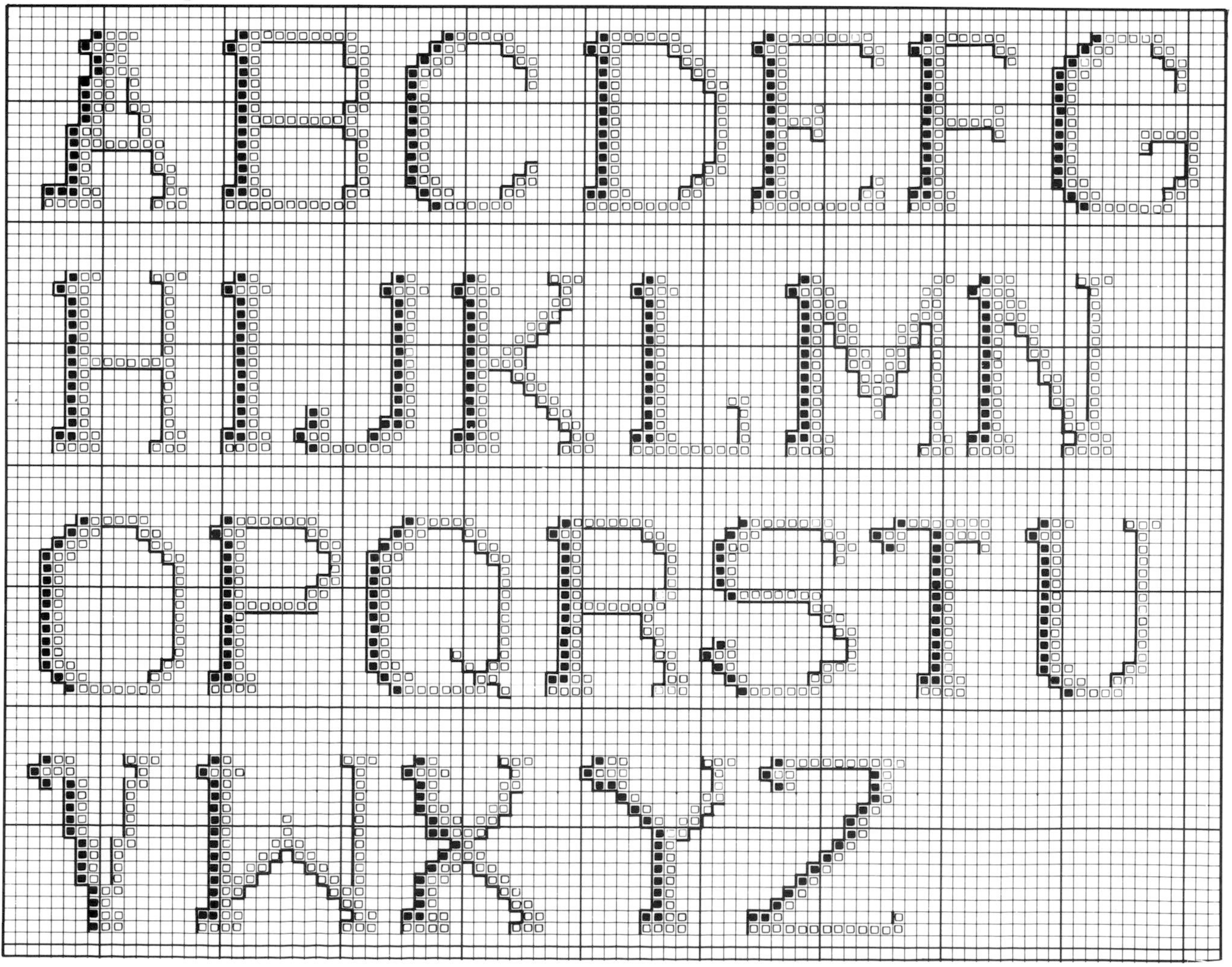

Stocking, bottom right

A
MIDNIGHT
CLEAR

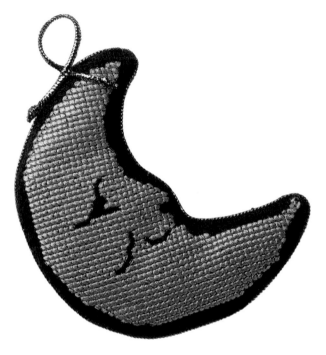

"It came upon a midnight clear."
So begins a favorite traditional
Christmas carol. Moon-lit and
star-brightened, this stocking
and set of ornaments recall that
silent night so long ago.
Edge them with gold to bring
a rich shimmer to your home
this holiday season.

STOCKING

SAMPLE
Stitched on navy Aida 11 over 1, the finished design size is 9⅞" x 9¾". The fabric was cut 17" x 20". See Suppliers for specialty thread.

FABRICS	DESIGN SIZES
Aida 14	7¾" x 7⅝"
Aida 18	6" x 6"
Hardanger 22	5" x 4⅞"

MATERIALS

- Completed cross-stitch; matching thread
- Dressmaker's pen
- 17" x 20" piece of un-stitched navy Aida 11
- ¾ yard of yellow jersey; matching thread
- Fusible interfacing
- 2½ yards of ⅛"-wide gold braided piping
- Seven medium-size jingle bells

DIRECTIONS
All seams are ¼".

1. Make cuff pattern. From yellow jersey, cut two cuff pieces. Also cut 2½" x 5" strip for hanger. Fuse interfacing to wrong side of both cuff pieces.

2. Stitch braided piping to edge of points on right side of one cuff piece to make cuff front (see Diagram 1 on page 31). With right sides together, stitch short ends of cuff; do not turn.

3. With right sides together, stitch short ends of remaining cuff piece to make cuff lining; turn right side out. Aligning seams and points, slide lining inside cuff front. Stitch lining to cuff front on pointed edge. Draw lining up out of cuff front and down, so raw edges align (see Diagram 2 on page 31). Turn cuff; press with lining on inside.

4. To complete cuff, turn in top raw edges of lining and cuff; slipstitch together. Set aside.

5. Make stocking pattern on page 32, subtracting 3¾" as indicated. With completed design horizontally centered on pattern and top of stitching 5¼" below stocking top, cut out one stocking. Also cut one stocking from unstitched Aida 11 for stocking back and two stockings from yellow jersey for lining, reversing patterns as needed.

6. Stitch braided piping to right side of design piece. With right sides together, stitch design piece to stocking back along stitching line of piping, leaving top open. Turn.

7. To make stocking lining, stitch yellow stockings with right sides together, leaving open at top and for 3" along seam above heel; do not turn. Slide lining over stocking, aligning top edges and seams. Stitch around stocking top. Pull stocking through opening in lining, turning right side out. Slipstitch opening closed. Tuck lining inside stocking.

8. To make hanger, stitch long edges of yellow strip. Turn. Press with seam in center.

9. Slide cuff over stocking with points down so cuff top is ¼" above stocking top and seam is centered on stocking back. Baste hanger to cuff back at heel seam of stocking. Hand-sew cuff to stocking, securing hanger.

10. Attach bells to cuff (see photo).

ORNAMENTS

SAMPLE
All three ornaments are stitched on navy Aida 11 over 1. The finished design size for the moon is 4½" x 4½". The fabric was cut 9" x 9". The finished design size for the small star is 2¼" x 2⅛". The fabric was cut 7" x 7". The finished design size for the large star is 2⅞" x 2¾". The fabric was cut 8" x 8". The motifs are taken from the Moon Stocking. See Suppliers for specialty thread.

Moon	
FABRICS	DESIGN SIZES
Aida 14	3½" x 3⅝"
Aida 18	2¾" x 2¾"
Hardanger 22	2¼" x 2¼"

Small Star	
FABRICS	DESIGN SIZES
Aida 14	2¼" x 2⅛"
Aida 18	1¾" x 1⅝"
Hardanger 22	1⅜" x 1⅜"

Large Star	
FABRICS	DESIGN SIZES
Aida 14	2⅞" x 2¾"
Aida 18	2¼" x 2⅛"
Hardanger 22	1⅞" x 1¾"

MATERIALS FOR ONE

- Completed cross-stitch; matching thread
- 6" x 6" piece of un-stitched navy Aida 11
- Polyester stuffing
- 24" of ⅛"-diameter gold cord or ¼"-wide gold rickrack
- Gold metallic thread

DIRECTIONS
All seams are ¼".

1. Trim completed design piece ½" from stitched area, following contour of motif. Using design piece as pattern, cut ornament back from unstitched Aida 11.

2. With right sides together, stitch design piece to back, aligning edges and leaving an opening. Turn. Stuff moderately. Slipstitch opening closed.

3. Using gold thread and beginning and ending at top, hand-sew gold cord or rickrack along ornament seam.

4. To make hanger, cut 6" length of gold cord. Knot ends. Make loop, criss-crossing ends ½" from knots (see photo). Tack to ornament front at top.

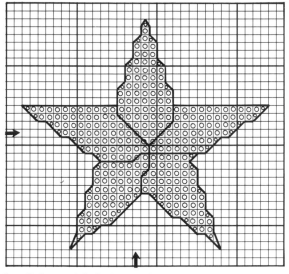

Small Star • Stitch Count: 31 x 29

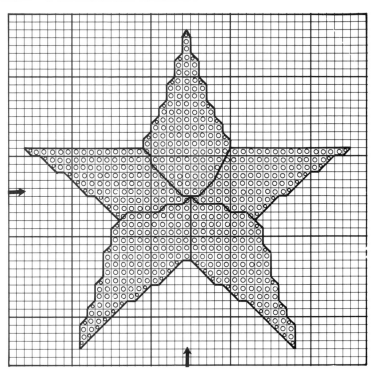

Large Star • Stitch Count: 41 x 39

Stocking and ornaments ★

DMC		Marlitt (used for sample)

Step 1: Cross-stitch (3 strands)

725		821	Topaz

Step 2: Backstitch (2 strands)

	2320	J&P Coats
		Copper Metallic

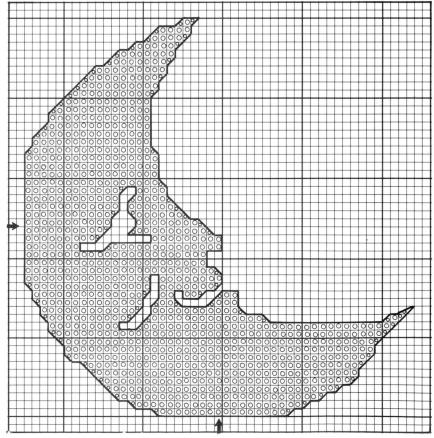

Moon • Stitch Count: 49 x 50

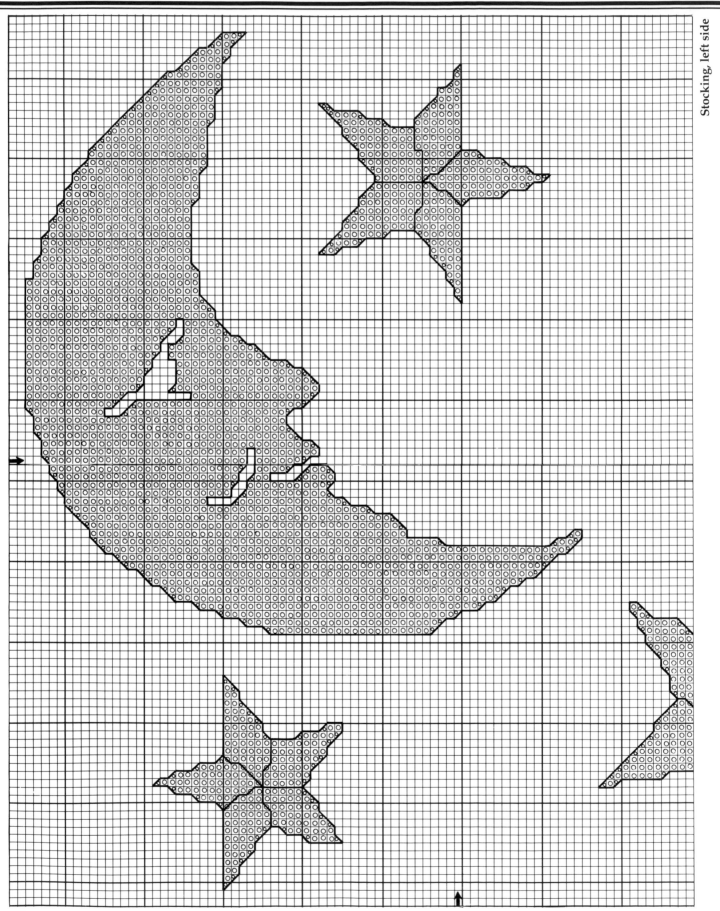

Stocking, left side

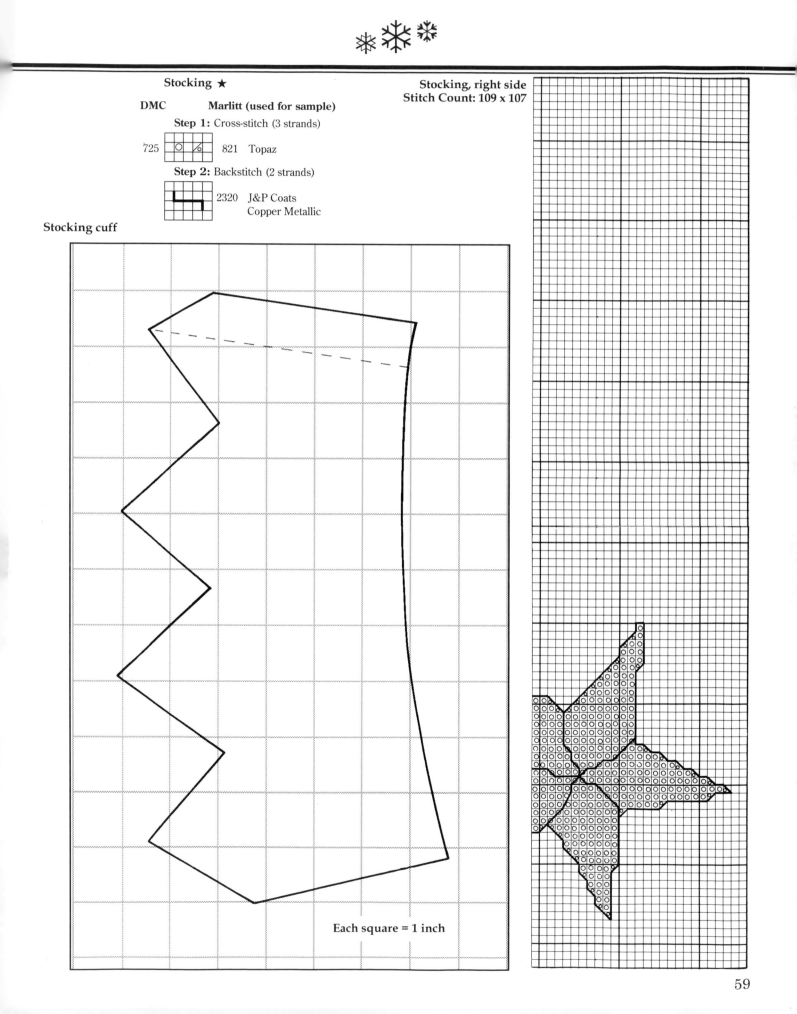

Stocking ★

DMC   **Marlitt (used for sample)**

Step 1: Cross-stitch (3 strands)

725   821   Topaz

Step 2: Backstitch (2 strands)

2320   J&P Coats
Copper Metallic

Stocking cuff

Each square = 1 inch

Stocking, right side
Stitch Count: 109 x 107

CHRISTMAS ANGELS

Love dwells in every stitch
of this angelic sampler.
The ornate matching swag
sends a host of angels fluttering
over mantel or door amid
clusters of Christmas stars.
You can almost hear their
sweet voices announcing
the glorious meaning of the season!

60

LOVE CAME DOWN AT CHRISTMAS
LOVE ALL LOVELY, LOVE DIVINE
LOVE WAS BORN AT CHRISTMAS
STAR AND ANGELS GAVE THEM SIGN.
CHRISTINA ROSSETTI

SAMPLER

SAMPLE
Stitched on white Aida 11 over 1, the finished design size is 17¾" x 14¾". The fabric was cut 24" x 21".

FABRICS	DESIGN SIZES
Aida 14	13⅞" x 11⅝"
Aida 18	10⅞" x 9"
Hardanger 22	8⅞" x 7⅜"

SWAG

SAMPLE
The swag motifs are stitched on white Aida 11 over 1. The finished design sizes are: 6⅞" x 4" for the right-facing angel (not shown in photo), 6¾" x 4" for left-facing and center angels and 2¾" x 3" for one star. The fabric for each angel was cut 11" x 9". The fabric for one star was cut 6" x 6". The swag motifs are taken from the Angel Sampler on pages 64-67; use the codes opposite. Stitch three angels and five stars, or repeat motifs to make swag as long as desired. Motifs may also be made into individual ornaments. See Suppliers for specialty thread and ribbon.

Right-facing Angel
FABRICS	DESIGN SIZES
Aida 14	5⅜" x 3⅛"
Aida 18	4⅛" x 2⅜"
Hardanger 22	3⅜" x 2"

Stitch Count: 75 x 43

Center, Left-facing Angels
FABRICS	DESIGN SIZES
Aida 14	5¼" x 3⅛"
Aida 18	4⅛" x 2⅜"
Hardanger 22	3⅜" x 2"

Stitch Count: 74 x 43

One Star
FABRICS	DESIGN SIZES
Aida 14	2⅛" x 2¼"
Aida 18	1⅝" x 1¾"
Hardanger 22	1⅜" x 1½"

Stitch Count: 30 x 32

MATERIALS

- 8 completed cross-stitch pieces
- ¼ yard of unstitched white Aida 11
- Dressmaker's pen
- Polyester stuffing
- Gold metallic or monofilament thread
- 10 yards (2 spools) of ⅛"-wide, gold metallic cord
- 7 yards of 1½"-wide pink wired ribbon with gold edging
- 4 yards of ⅞"-wide pink wired ribbon with gold edging
- 4 yards of ⅞"-wide raspberry wired ribbon with gold edging
- 6 yards of 3/16"-wide gold metallic ribbon
- Craft wire
- White thread

DIRECTIONS
All seams are ¼".

1. Trim each completed design piece ½" from stitched area, following contour of motif (see photo). Using design pieces as patterns, cut one matching back for each motif from unstitched Aida 11.

2. With right sides together, stitch a back to each design piece, aligning edges and leaving an opening. Turn. Stuff firmly. Slipstitch each opening closed.

3. Using gold metallic or monofilament thread, hand-sew gold cord around each swag piece, following seam.

4. Using white thread, tack three stars together (see photo). Set star cluster and remaining swag pieces aside.

5. To make a small bow, cut one 24" length each from ⅞"-wide pink and raspberry ribbons and 3/16"-wide gold metallic ribbon. Handling lengths as one, tie a bow. Notch ends of pink and raspberry ribbons. Trim ends of gold metallic ribbon diagonally. Repeat to make seven bows.

6. Tack small bows, angels, and stars along length of remaining 1½"-wide pink ribbon, beginning 28" from one end in the following order, or as desired: bow, star, bow, right-facing angel, bow, cluster of three stars, bow, center angel (pink gown), bow, star, left-facing angel (purple-edged gown), bow, star, bow.

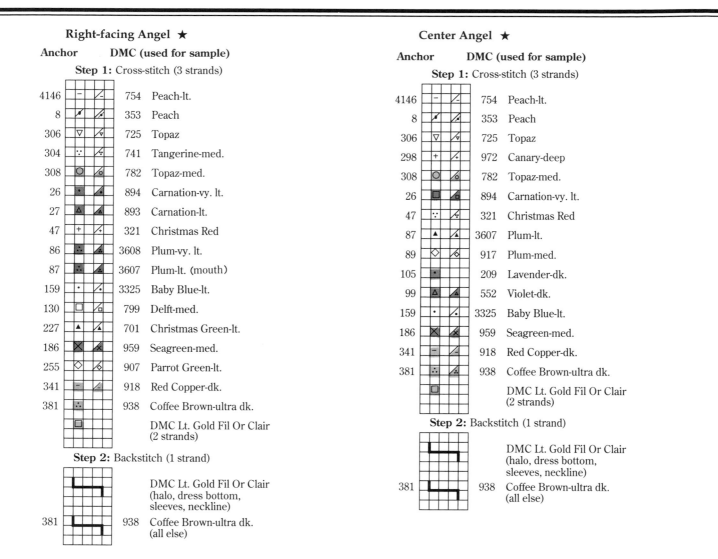

Right-facing Angel ★

Anchor			DMC (used for sample)	
Step 1: Cross-stitch (3 strands)				
4146	–		754	Peach-lt.
8			353	Peach
306	▽		725	Topaz
304	⋰		741	Tangerine-med.
308	○		782	Topaz-med.
26	▪		894	Carnation-vy. lt.
27	▲		893	Carnation-lt.
47	+		321	Christmas Red
86	⋮		3608	Plum-vy. lt.
87	⋮		3607	Plum-lt. (mouth)
159	·		3325	Baby Blue-lt.
130	□		799	Delft-med.
227	▲		701	Christmas Green-lt.
186	✕		959	Seagreen-med.
255	◇		907	Parrot Green-lt.
341	▭		918	Red Copper-dk.
381	⋰		938	Coffee Brown-ultra dk.
	□			DMC Lt. Gold Fil Or Clair (2 strands)

Step 2: Backstitch (1 strand)

				DMC Lt. Gold Fil Or Clair (halo, dress bottom, sleeves, neckline)
381			938	Coffee Brown-ultra dk. (all else)

Center Angel ★

Anchor			DMC (used for sample)	
Step 1: Cross-stitch (3 strands)				
4146	–		754	Peach-lt.
8			353	Peach
306	▽		725	Topaz
298	+		972	Canary-deep
308	○		782	Topaz-med.
26	□		894	Carnation-vy. lt.
47	⋰		321	Christmas Red
87	▲		3607	Plum-lt.
89	◇		917	Plum-med.
105	▪		209	Lavender-dk.
99	▲		552	Violet-dk.
159	·		3325	Baby Blue-lt.
186	✕		959	Seagreen-med.
341			918	Red Copper-dk.
381	⋰		938	Coffee Brown-ultra dk.
	□			DMC Lt. Gold Fil Or Clair (2 strands)

Step 2: Backstitch (1 strand)

				DMC Lt. Gold Fil Or Clair (halo, dress bottom, sleeves, neckline)
381			938	Coffee Brown-ultra dk. (all else)

Left-facing Angel ★

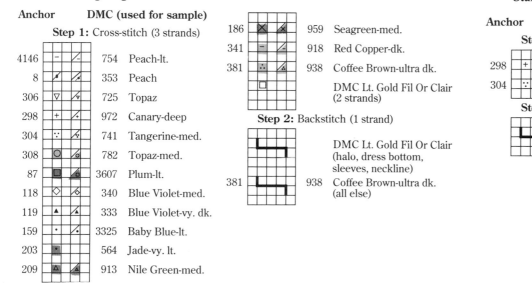

Anchor			DMC (used for sample)	
Step 1: Cross-stitch (3 strands)				
4146	–		754	Peach-lt.
8			353	Peach
306	▽		725	Topaz
298	+		972	Canary-deep
304	⋰		741	Tangerine-med.
308	○		782	Topaz-med.
87	□		3607	Plum-lt.
118	◇		340	Blue Violet-med.
119	▲		333	Blue Violet-vy. dk.
159	·		3325	Baby Blue-lt.
203	▪		564	Jade-vy. lt.
209	▲		913	Nile Green-med.
186	✕		959	Seagreen-med.
341			918	Red Copper-dk.
381	⋰		938	Coffee Brown-ultra dk.
	□			DMC Lt. Gold Fil Or Clair (2 strands)

Step 2: Backstitch (1 strand)

				DMC Lt. Gold Fil Or Clair (halo, dress bottom, sleeves, neckline)
381			938	Coffee Brown-ultra dk. (all else)

Star ★

Anchor			DMC (used for sample)	
Step 1: Cross-stitch (2 strands)				
298	+		972	Canary-deep
304	⋰		741	Tangerine-med.

Step 2: Backstitch (1 strand)

			DMC Lt. Gold Fil Or Clair

CHRISTMAS ANGELS

Sampler ★

Anchor			DMC	(used for sample)

Step 1: Cross-stitch (3 strands)

Anchor			DMC	
4146	−	⁄	754	Peach-lt.
8	⁄	⁄	353	Peach
306	▽	▽	725	Topaz
298	+	⁄	972	Canary-deep
304	∴	⁄	741	Tangerine-med.
308	○	⁄	782	Topaz-med.
26	▯	⁄	894	Carnation-vy. lt.
27	∷	⁄	893	Carnation-lt.
47	✕		321	Christmas Red
85	⌁	⁄	3609	Plum-ultra lt.
86	✕		3608	Plum-vy. lt.
87	▫	⁄	3607	Plum-lt.

Anchor			DMC	
89	■		917	Plum-med.
105	·		209	Lavender-dk.
99	△		552	Violet-dk.
118	◇	◈	340	Blue Violet-med.
119	▲	⁄	333	Blue Violet-vy. dk.
159	·	⁄	3325	Baby Blue-lt.
130	□	◸	799	Delft-med.
134	◆	⁄	820	Royal Blue-vy. dk.
203	▪	▪	564	Jade-vy. lt.
209	△	⁄	913	Nile Green-med.
227	●		701	Christmas Green-lt.
186	✕	✕	959	Seagreen-med.
255	○		907	Parrot Green-lt.
341		⁄	918	Red Copper-dk.

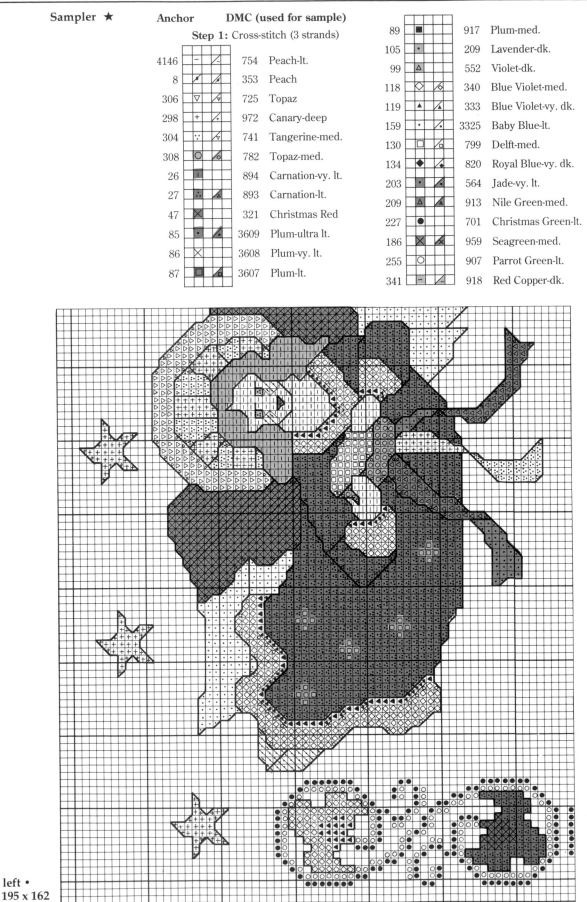

Sampler , top left •
Stitch Count: 195 x 162

64

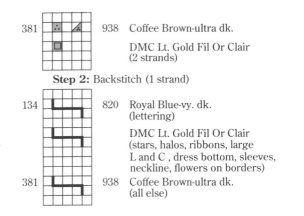

| 381 | 938 | Coffee Brown-ultra dk. |
| | | DMC Lt. Gold Fil Or Clair (2 strands) |

Step 2: Backstitch (1 strand)

134	820	Royal Blue-vy. dk. (lettering)
		DMC Lt. Gold Fil Or Clair (stars, halos, ribbons, large L and C , dress bottom, sleeves, neckline, flowers on borders)
381	938	Coffee Brown-ultra dk. (all else)

Sampler, bottom left

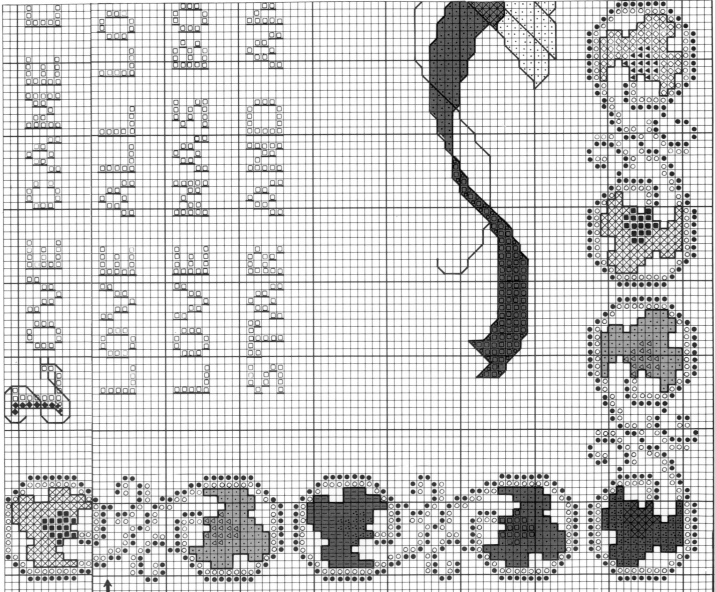

Sampler, top right

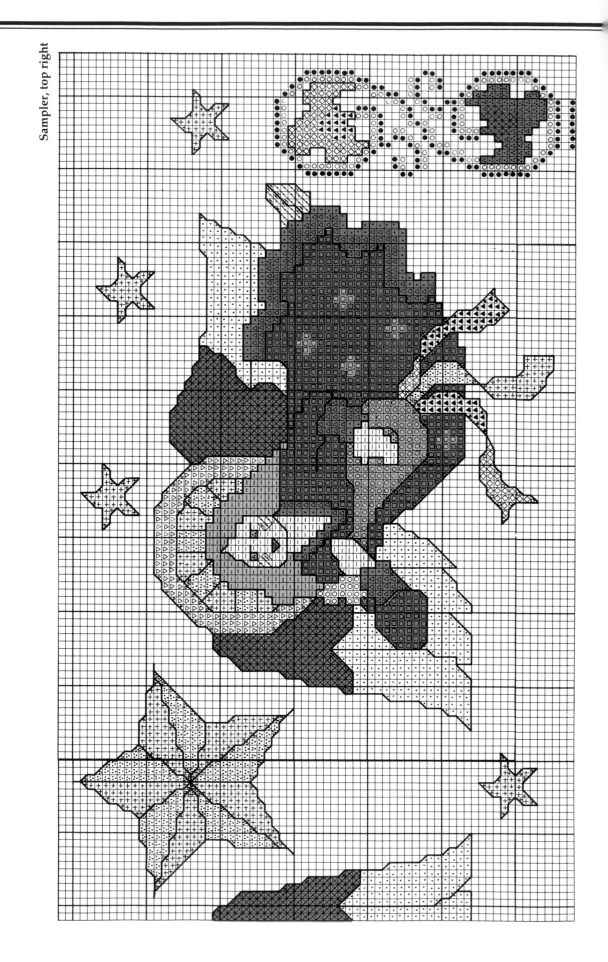

CALICO CHRISTMAS

Crisp and cheerful,
calico patchwork is a wonderful
companion for these country-fresh
cross-stitched designs.
The pieced hanging adds warmth
and brightness to any wall,
while the throw pillows
enliven a sofa or chair.
Piece your prettiest
fabric scraps to finish these projects
in colorful style.

WALL HANGING

SAMPLE

All four motifs are stitched on white Aida 14 over 1. The finished design size for Motif 1 is 7⅞" x 7⅞". The finished design size for Motifs 2, 3 and 4 is 7¾" x 7¾". The fabric for each motif was cut 15" x 15" Each graph shows ¼ of each design. See the Assembly Diagram before beginning to stitch.

Motif 1

FABRICS	DESIGN SIZES
Aida 11	10" x 10"
Aida 18	6⅛" x 6⅛"
Hardanger 22	5" x 5"

Motifs 2 and 3

FABRICS	DESIGN SIZES
Aida 11	9⅞" x 9⅞"
Aida 18	6" x 6"
Hardanger 22	4⅞" x 4⅞"

Motif 4

FABRICS	DESIGN SIZES
Aida 11	9⅞" x 9⅞"
Aida 18	6" x 6"
Hardanger 22	5" x 4⅞"

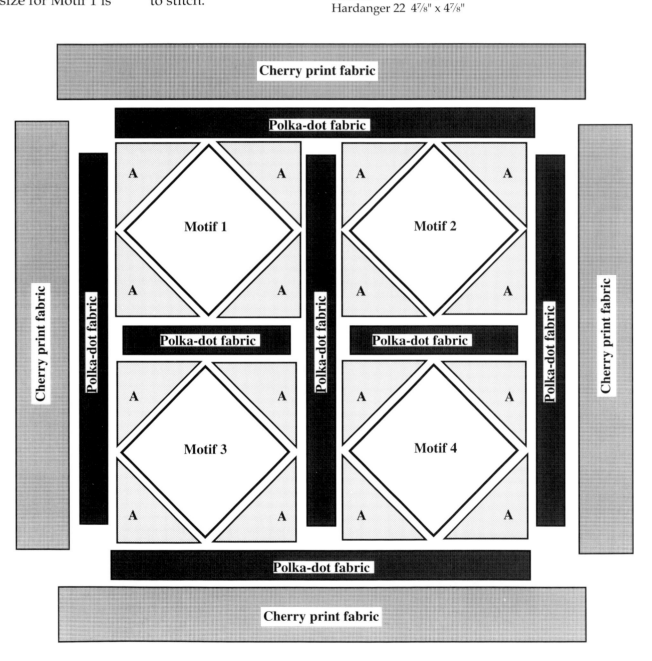

Wall Hanging Assembly Diagram

MATERIALS

- 4 completed cross-stitch pieces
- Dressmaker's pen
- 2⅛ yards of green print fabric
- ⅜ yard of red/white polka-dot fabric
- ⅜ yard of cherry print fabric
- Matching threads for fabrics
- 42" x 44" piece of fleece
- 3 pieces of fleece, each 9" x 4"

DIRECTIONS

All seams are ¼".

1. With completed designs centered, trim design pieces to 9¾" x 9¾" each. Zigzag edges.

2. From green print fabric, cut 16 of Template A for block corners, aligning fabric grain with arrows on pattern, and one 40½" x 40½" piece for wall hanging back. Set back aside.

3. From red/white polka-dot fabric, cut the following: two 33¼" x 2¾" pieces; three 28¾" x 2⅞" pieces; two 13¼" x 2¾" pieces. Also cut 3¼"-wide bias strips, piecing as needed to make 4¾ yards of binding; set binding aside.

4. From cherry print fabric, cut the following: two 40½" x 4" pieces;

two 34¼" x 4" pieces; three 9" x 4" pieces for hangers. Set hangers aside.

Refer to Assembly Diagram for Steps 5-9.

5. Stitch one A piece to each edge of each design piece to make motif blocks.

6. Stitch the long edges of one 13¼" x 2¾" polka-dot piece between Motifs 1 and 3; stitch the other between motifs 2 and 4.

7. Stitch the long edges of one 28¾" x 2⅞" polka-dot piece between the assembled Motifs 1-3 and 2-4. Stitch one long edge of remaining 28¾" x 2⅞" polka-dot pieces to each of the outside vertical edges of the assembled motifs.

8. To complete wall hanging center, stitch remaining polka-dot pieces to top and bottom edges.

9. To complete wall hanging top, stitch one 34¼" x 4" cherry print piece to each side edge of wall hanging center, aligning the top and bottom edges. Stitch one 40½" x 4" cherry print piece to top and bottom edges of wall hanging center.

10. Layer wall hanging back wrong side up, 42" x 44" fleece piece and wall hanging top right side up. Baste. Trim the fleece from seam allowance. Using green thread, machine-quilt along seams or as desired.

11. Bind wall hanging with polka-dot binding, mitering corners.

12. To make one hanger, baste a 9" x 4" piece of fleece to wrong side of one cherry print hanger piece. With right sides together, stitch long edges. Trim fleece from seam allowance. Turn. With seam in center, press. Make loop with seam to inside. Turn ends to inside, also; baste together (see Diagram 2). Repeat to make two more hangers. Tack one hanger to back at top right, top left, and top center.

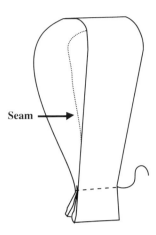

Seam →

Diagram 2

PILLOWS

SAMPLE

All three pillows are stitched on white Aida 14 over 1. The fabric for each was cut 15" x 15". The motifs are taken from the Wall Hanging on pages 73–75 and use the same code. Directions given are for the small red-bordered pillow and the large pillow; substitute other colors as shown or as desired to vary the borders.

SMALL PILLOW MATERIALS

- Completed cross-stitch
- Dressmaker's pen
- 4 squares of green plaid fabric, each 2¼" x 2¼"
- 2 strips of medium red fabric, each 10½" x 2¼"
- 2 strips of dark red fabric, each 10½" x 2¼"
- ⅝ yard of dark red fabric for back and piping
- Thread to match fabrics
- 2 yards of ¼"-diameter cotton cording
- Polyester stuffing

DIRECTIONS

All seams are ¼"

1. With the completed design centered, trim design piece to 10½" x 10½".

2. Stitch one green plaid square to each end of two matching 10½"-long red strips (see Diagram 1).

3. Stitch remaining red strips to opposite edges of design piece. Stitch strips with green squares to remaining edges of design piece, completing pillow front (see Diagram 2).

4. Using pillow front as pattern, cut pillow back from dark red fabric. Also cut 1¼"-wide bias strips, piecing as needed to equal 2 yards.

5. Cover the cotton cord with the bias strip to make corded piping. Beginning and ending in middle of one edge, stitch piping to right side of pillow front, finishing piping ends neatly.

6. With right sides together, stitch pillow front to pillow back, leaving opening in middle of one edge. Turn. Stuff moderately. Slipstitch opening closed.

Diagram 1

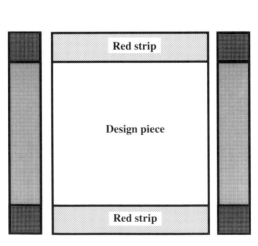

Red strip

Design piece

Red strip

Diagram 2

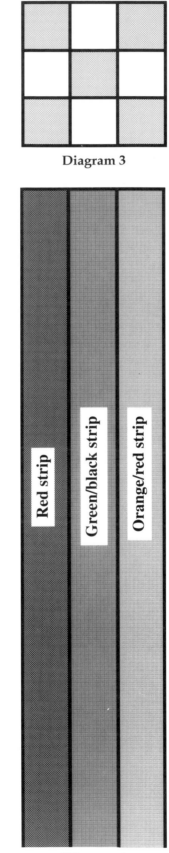

Red strip

Green/black strip

Orange/red strip

Diagram 3

Diagram 4

LARGE PILLOW MATERIALS

- Completed cross-stitch
- Dressmaker's pen
- 20 squares dark red fabric, each 1¼" x 1¼"
- 16 squares green/white fabric, each 1¼" x 1¼"
- 4 strips red/red fabric, each 10½" x 1¼"
- 4 strips orange/red fabric, each 10½" x 1¼"
- 4 strips green/black fabric, each 10½" x 1¼"
- ⅝ yard of green/black fabric
- Thread to match fabrics
- 2 yards of ¼"-diameter cotton cording
- Polyester stuffing

DIRECTIONS
All seams are ¼".

1. With completed design centered, trim the design piece to 10½" x 10½".

2. Arrange five dark red squares and four green/white squares as shown in Diagram 3. Sew together in rows, then sew rows together. Repeat to make four corner blocks.

3. Stitch a red/red, a green/black and an orange/red strip togeth-er as shown in Diagram 4. Repeat to make four border strips.

4. Stitch one corner block to each end of two border strips, matching seams.

5. Stitch red/red edges of remaining border strips to opposite edges of design piece. Stitch red/red edges of strips with corner blocks to remaining edges of design piece, completing pillow front.

6. Using remaining green/black fabric, fol-low Steps 4-6 of Small Pillow, opposite page, to complete large pillow.

Motif 1 • Stitch Count: 110 x 110   one quarter of design

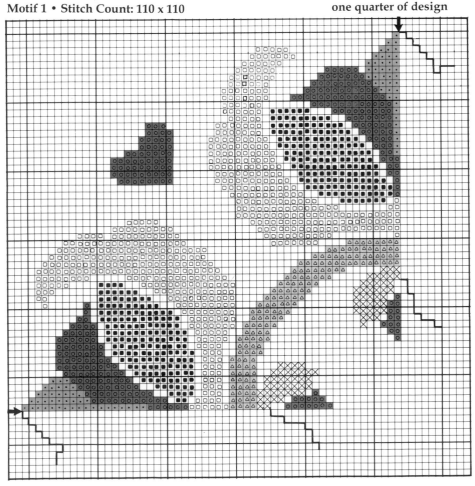

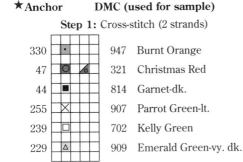

★ Anchor   DMC (used for sample)

Step 1: Cross-stitch (2 strands)

Anchor		DMC	
330	•	947	Burnt Orange
47	◯ ⁄	321	Christmas Red
44	■	814	Garnet-dk.
255	✕	907	Parrot Green-lt.
239	☐	702	Kelly Green
229	△	909	Emerald Green-vy. dk.

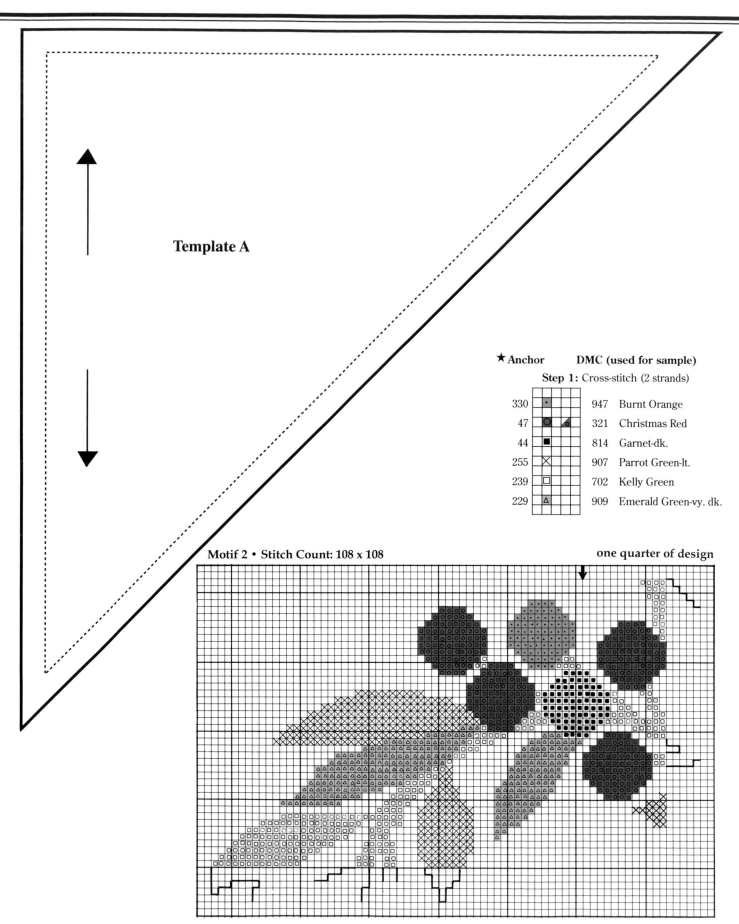

Template A

★ **Anchor**   **DMC (used for sample)**

Step 1: Cross-stitch (2 strands)

Anchor		DMC	
330	·	947	Burnt Orange
47	◐ ◢	321	Christmas Red
44	■	814	Garnet-dk.
255	✕	907	Parrot Green-lt.
239	□	702	Kelly Green
229	△	909	Emerald Green-vy. dk.

Motif 2 • Stitch Count: 108 x 108   one quarter of design

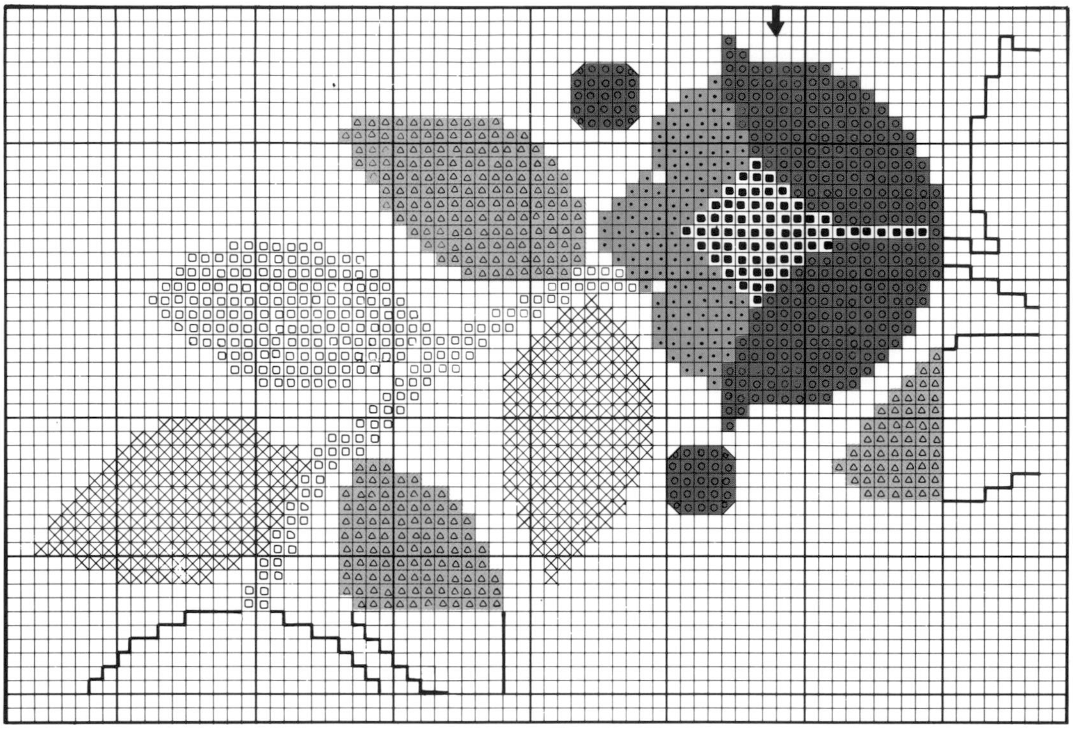

Motif 3 • Stitch Count: 108 x 108

one quarter of design

Motif 4 • Stitch Count: 108 x 108

one quarter of design

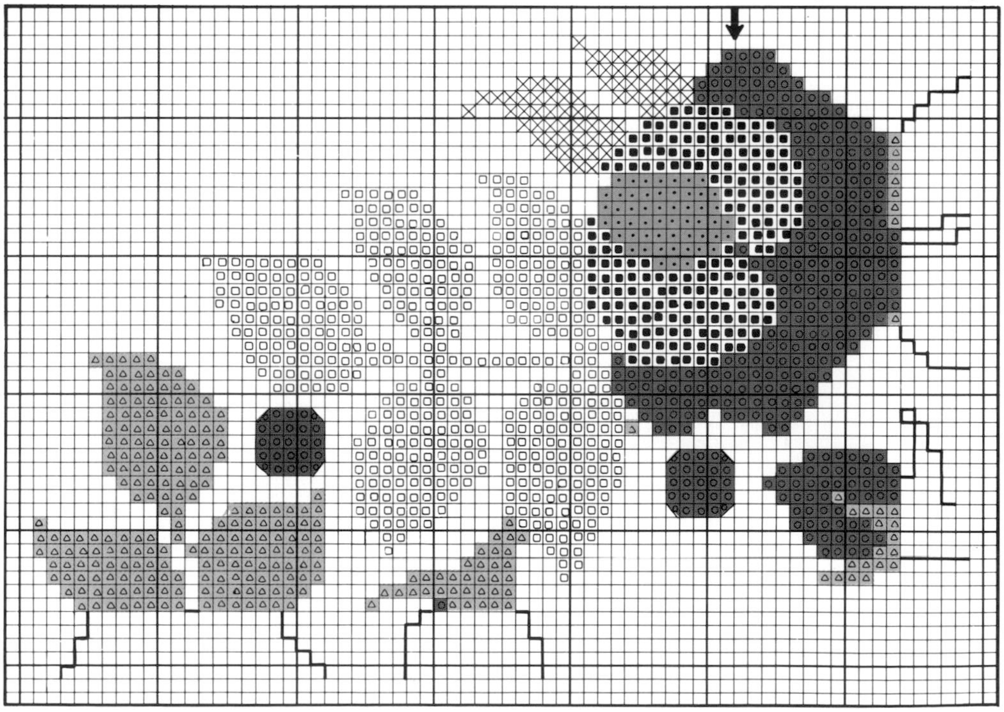

S M A L L
T R E A S U R E S

Gifts of love weave Christmas magic.
Here is a wealth of small treasures
to create for holiday giving.
Stitch this personalized sampler
stocking, then fill it with
the handmade hair bows,
bookmarks and other treats.
Cross-stitched gift tags are sure
to be cherished long after packages
are opened. And what fashionable
toddler could resist
the charmingly decorated
pinafore or overalls?

STOCKING

CUFF SAMPLE
Stitched on delft blue Aida 14 over 1, the finished design size is 6³/₈" x 2³/₈". If the name to be stitched is too long to fit the design, stitch initials only. The fabric was cut 18" x 9".

FABRICS	DESIGN SIZES
Aida 11	8¹/₈" x 3"
Aida 18	5" x 1⁷/₈"
Hardanger 22	4¹/₈" x 1¹/₂"

CUFF MATERIALS

- Completed cross-stitch; matching thread
- 17¹/₂" x 3¹/₄" piece of un-stitched delft blue Aida 14
- ¹/₈ yard of red broadcloth
- ⁷/₈ yard of ¹/₈"-diameter cotton cording

DIRECTIONS
All seams are ¹/₄".

1. Trim left side of completed design piece 1" from stitched border design. With design centered, trim cuff to 3¹/₄" deep. Using design piece as pattern, cut matching piece from unstitched Aida 14 for cuff lining.

2. From red broadcloth, cut 1¹/₄"-wide bias strips, piecing as needed to equal 25". Make corded piping.

3. Cut piping in half. Stitch one length to right side of each long edge of cuff (see Diagram 1 on page 31). With right sides together, stitch short ends of cuff; do not turn.

4. With right sides together, stitch short ends of cuff lining; turn right side out. Aligning seams, slide lining inside design piece. Stitch top edge of lining to design piece along stitching line of piping. Draw lining up out of design piece and down, so bottom edges align (see Diagram 2 on page 31). Turn cuff; press with lining on inside.

5. To complete cuff, turn in raw edges of lining and cuff; slipstitch together. Set aside.

STOCKING SAMPLE
Stitched on delft blue Aida 14 over 1, the finished design size is 8⁵/₈" x 11³/₄". The fabric was cut 13" x 19".

FABRICS	DESIGN SIZES
Aida 11	10⁷/₈" x 14⁷/₈"
Aida 18	6⁵/₈" x 9¹/₈"
Hardanger 22	5¹/₂" x 7¹/₂"

STOCKING MATERIALS

- Completed cross-stitch; matching thread
- 13" x 19" piece of un-stitched delft blue Aida 14
- ³/₈ yard of blue cotton fabric
- ³/₈ yard of fleece
- 1¹/₂ yards of ¹/₈"-diameter cotton cording
- ¹/₄ yard of red broadcloth
- Completed stocking cuff

DIRECTIONS
All seams are ¹/₄".

1. Following contours of design, trim completed design piece ¹/₂" from stitched area on sides and bottom and 3" from stitched area at top. Using design piece as pattern, cut one stocking back from unstitched Aida 14. From blue fabric, cut two stockings for lining, reversing pattern for one if needed. From fleece, cut two stockings.

2. From red broadcloth, cut 1¹/₄"-wide bias strips, piecing as needed to equal 1 yard of piping. Make corded piping.

3. Stitch piping to right side of design piece. Matching edges, baste one fleece stocking to wrong side of design piece. Baste remaining fleece stocking to wrong side of stocking back.

4. With right sides together, stitch stocking back to design piece along stitching line of piping, leaving top open. Trim fleece from seam allowance. Turn.

5. To make stocking lining, stitch blue fabric stockings with right sides together, leaving open at top and for 3" along seam above heel; do not turn. Slide lining over stocking, aligning top edges and seams. Stitch around stocking top. Pull stocking through opening in lining, turning right side out. Slipstitch opening closed. Tuck lining inside stocking.

6. To make hanger, cut 1¹/₂" x 5" strip from un-stitched Aida 14. Stitch long edges. Turn. Press with seam in center. Fold hanger in half and baste outside stocking at top beside heel seam.

7. Slide cuff over stocking so piping on top edge is slightly above stocking top and seam aligns with stocking heel seam, centering design on stocking front; see photo. Hand-sew cuff to stocking, securing hanger.

GIFT TAG

SAMPLE
Stitched on cream Perforated Paper 14 over 1, the finished design size is determined by the length of the name stitched. The design size of the sample is 4¹/₂" x 1⁷/₈". Cut the paper to allow at least 2" around the design.

FABRICS	DESIGN SIZES
Aida 11	5⁵/₈" x 2"
Aida 14	4¹/₂" x 1⁷/₈"
Aida 18	3¹/₂" x 1¹/₂"
Hardanger 22	2⁷/₈" x 1¹/₈"

MATERIALS

- Completed cross-stitch
- Tracing paper
- Pencil
- Cardboard
- Spray adhesive
- Craft knife

- 8" length of thin gold cord
- Needle

DIRECTIONS

1. Trace gift tag pattern, adding length as needed to accommodate name.

2. Keeping design vertically centered and last letter of name ¼" from the short straight edge, transfer pattern to completed design piece. Trim design piece ¼" from pattern outline.

3. Coat surface of cardboard with spray adhesive. Press design piece onto cardboard. Using craft knife, cut out along pattern outline.

4. To make tag tie, thread needle with gold cord (see Diagram 1 on page 24). Insert needle through ornament near left edge (see photo). Complete tag tie (see Diagram 2 on page 24). Do not knot ends.

Gift Tag Pattern

Add to measurement here
to accommodate name

One Motif
FABRICS	DESIGN SIZES
Aida 11	1¾" x 3⅛"
Aida 18	1" x 2"
Hardanger 22	⅞" x 1⅝"

MATERIALS

- Completed cross-stitch; matching thread
- Overalls

DIRECTIONS

1. Before stitching design, measure overalls bib horizontally where placement is desired. Cut fabric 4" x horizontal

measurement, plus 3". Begin stitching first motif in center of fabric. Stitch to fill horizontal measurement.

2. Trim edges of completed design piece ¼" from stitched area. Zigzag edges.

3. Center design on overalls bib; pin at center only. Turn edges under; press, then pin.

4. Slipstitch design piece to overalls bib.

OVERALLS

SAMPLE
Stitched on black Aida 14 over 1, the finished design size is 1⅜" x 2½" for 1 motif. The motif is taken from the Sampler Stocking on pages 84-89; use the code on page 83. See Step 1 of directions before cutting and stitching fabric.

PINAFORE

SAMPLE
Stitched on black Aida 14 over 1, the finished design size is 3⅝" x 3¼" for 1 motif. The motif is taken from the Sampler Stocking on pages 84-89; use the code on page 82. See Step 1 of directions before stitching and cutting fabric.

One Motif
FABRICS	DESIGN SIZES
Aida 11	4½" x 4⅛"
Aida 18	2¾" x 2½"
Hardanger 22	2¼" x 2"

MATERIALS

- Completed cross-stitch; matching thread
- Pinafore

DIRECTIONS

1. Before stitching design, measure pinafore bib horizontally where placement is desired. Cut fabric 6" x measurement, plus 3". Begin stitching first motif in center of fabric. Stitch to fill horizontal measurement.

2. Follow Steps 2-4 of overalls, opposite.

HAIR BOWS

SAMPLE
Both hair bows are stitched on white Ribband 14 over 1. The motif for the holly hair bow is taken from the Sampler Stocking on pages 84-89 and uses the same code. The motif for the floral hair bow is taken from the Sampler Stocking Cuff on pages 84-85 and uses the same code. See Step 1 of the directions before cutting and stitching the ribbon. See Suppliers for specialty ribbon.

MATERIALS FOR BOTH

• 2¼ yards of ¾"-wide white Ribband 14
• Liquid ravel preventer
• White thread
• Two sew-on hair clips

DIRECTIONS

1. For holly hair bow, cut one 34½" and one 8½" length of Ribband 14. Beginning in center of each, stitch holly motifs to fill. For floral hair bow, cut one 31" and one 7" length of Ribband 14. Beginning in center of each, stitch floral motifs to fill.

2. To make hair bows, tie longer ribbon into a bow. Before tightening knot, insert shorter length through knot to make second set of tails. Trim tails of holly bow diagonally, tails of floral bow into wedge (see photo). Treat ends with liquid ravel preventer. At back of bows, pinch and fold over ribbon of knot to tighten; hand-sew in place.

3. Hand-sew one hair clip to each bow back.

BOOKMARKS

SNOWMAN SAMPLE
Stitched on delft blue Aida 14 over 1, the finished design size is 1¾" x 6⅛". The fabric was cut 6" x 11".

FABRICS	DESIGN SIZES
Aida 11	2⅛" x 7⅞"
Aida 18	1⅜" x 4¾"
Hardanger 22	1⅛" x 3⅞"

SNOWMAN MATERIALS

• Completed cross-stitch; matching thread

DIRECTIONS
All seams are ¼".

1. Trim completed design piece to 6" x 9". Zigzag long edges.

2. To make fringe, pull horizontal threads from short edges, stopping one row before design.

3. With right sides together, stitch long edges 1½" from design. Trim edges. Turn.

4. With design centered on front of bookmark and seam centered on back, press.

5. Stitch across each short edge above fringe, butting but not over, the design.

PINWHEEL CANDY SAMPLE
Stitched on white Aida 14 over 1, the finished design size is 1½" x 6⅛". The fabric was cut 6" x 11".

FABRICS	DESIGN SIZES
Aida 11	1⅞" x 7¾"
Aida 18	1⅛" x 4¾"
Hardanger 22	1" x 3⅞"

PINWHEEL CANDY MATERIALS

• Completed cross-stitch; matching thread

DIRECTIONS

1. Trim design piece to 4" x 9". Zigzag long edges.

2. Follow Step 2 of Snowman Bookmark.

3. With right sides together, stitch long edges ¾" from design. Trim edges. Turn.

4. Follow Steps 4-5 of Snowman Bookmark.

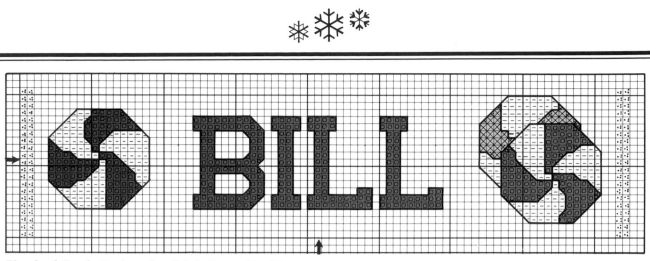

Pinwheel Candy Bookmark • Stitch Count: 21 x 85

Pinwheel Candy ★★

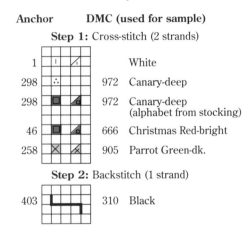

Anchor		DMC (used for sample)
		Step 1: Cross-stitch (2 strands)
1		White
298		972 Canary-deep
298		972 Canary-deep (alphabet from stocking)
46		666 Christmas Red-bright
258		905 Parrot Green-dk.
		Step 2: Backstitch (1 strand)
403		310 Black

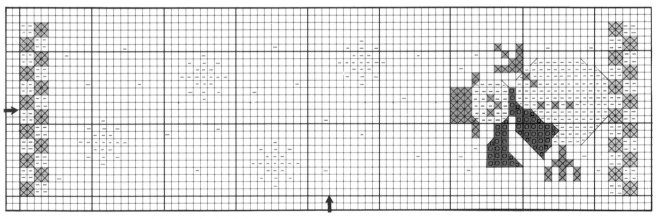

Snowman Bookmark • Stitch Count: 24 x 86

Snowman ★★

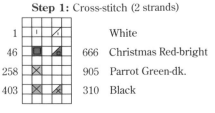

Anchor		DMC (used for sample)
		Step 1: Cross-stitch (2 strands)
1		White
46		666 Christmas Red-bright
258		905 Parrot Green-dk.
403		310 Black

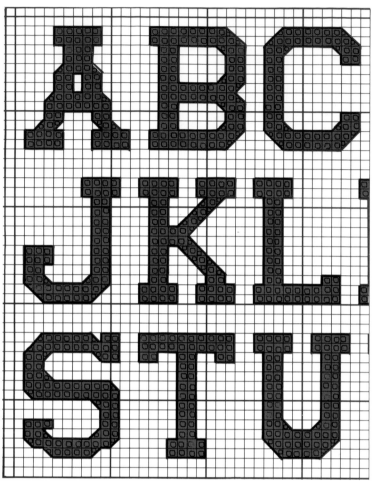

Alphabet

One Angel Motif • Stitch Count: 51 x 45

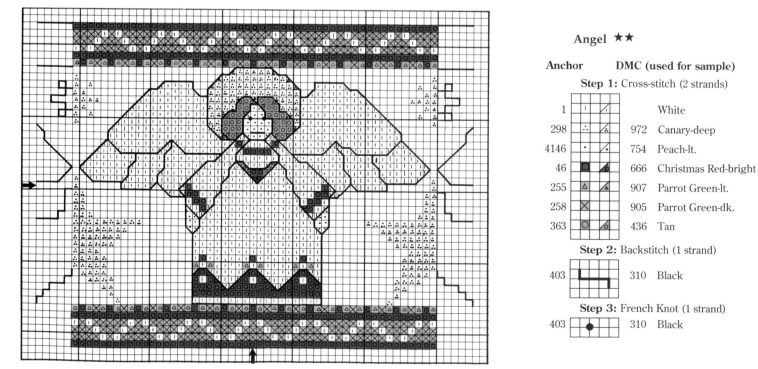

Angel ★★

Anchor   **DMC (used for sample)**

Step 1: Cross-stitch (2 strands)

Anchor		DMC	
1			White
298		972	Canary-deep
4146		754	Peach-lt.
46		666	Christmas Red-bright
255		907	Parrot Green-lt.
258		905	Parrot Green-dk.
363		436	Tan

Step 2: Backstitch (1 strand)

403		310	Black

Step 3: French Knot (1 strand)

403		310	Black

DEFGHI
MNOPQR
VWXYZ

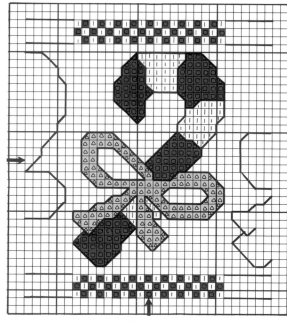

One Candy Cane Motif • Stitch Count: 19 x 35

Candy cane ★★

Anchor			DMC (used for sample)	

Step 1: Cross-stitch (2 strands)

1				White
46			666	Christmas Red-bright
255			907	Parrot Green-lt.

Step 2: Backstitch (1 strand)

403		310	Black

Gift Tag ★★

Anchor		DMC (used for sample)	

Step 1: Cross-stitch (2 strands)

1	ı		White
46	■	666	Christmas Red-bright
258	✕	905	Parrot Green-dk.

Step 2: Backstitch (1 strand)

| 403 | | 310 | Black |

Sampler, Stocking and Cuff ★★

Anchor		DMC (used for sample)	

Step 1: Cross-stitch (2 strands)

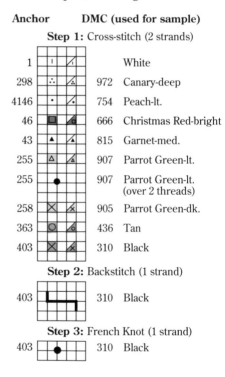

1	ı ╱		White
298	∴ ◹	972	Canary-deep
4146	• ◹	754	Peach-lt.
46	■ �￢	666	Christmas Red-bright
43	▲ ◹	815	Garnet-med.
255	△ ◹	907	Parrot Green-lt.
255	●	907	Parrot Green-lt. (over 2 threads)
258	✕ ◹	905	Parrot Green-dk.
363	◯ ◢	436	Tan
403	✕ ◹	310	Black

Step 2: Backstitch (1 strand)

| 403 | | 310 | Black |

Step 3: French Knot (1 strand)

| 403 | ● | 310 | Black |

Sampler Stocking Cuff • Stitch Count: 90 x 33

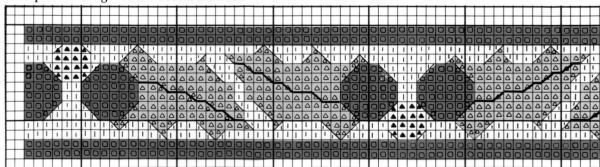

Sampler Stocking • Stitch Count: 120 x 164

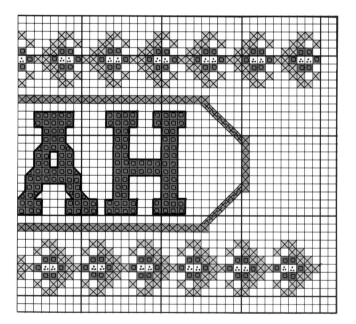

Gift Tag • Stitch Count: 62 x 26

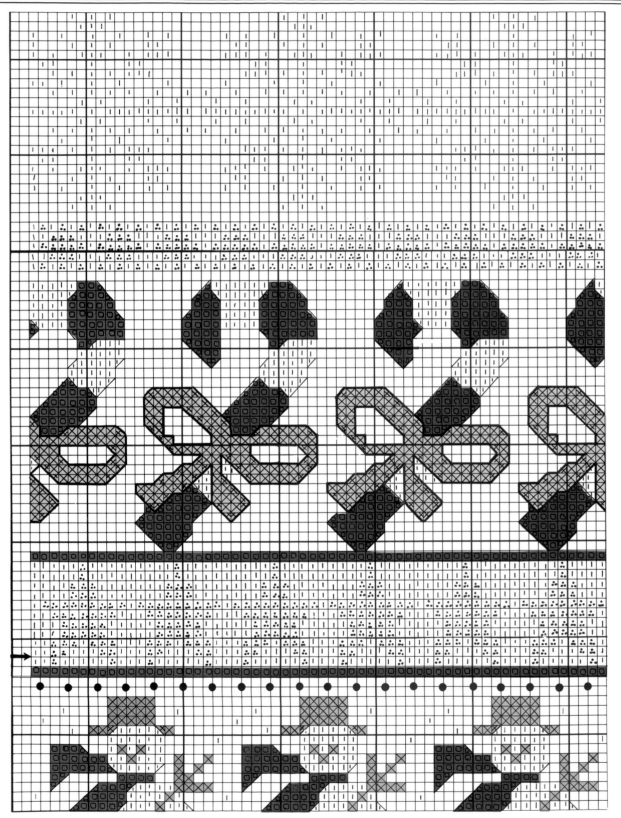

Sampler Stocking, top left

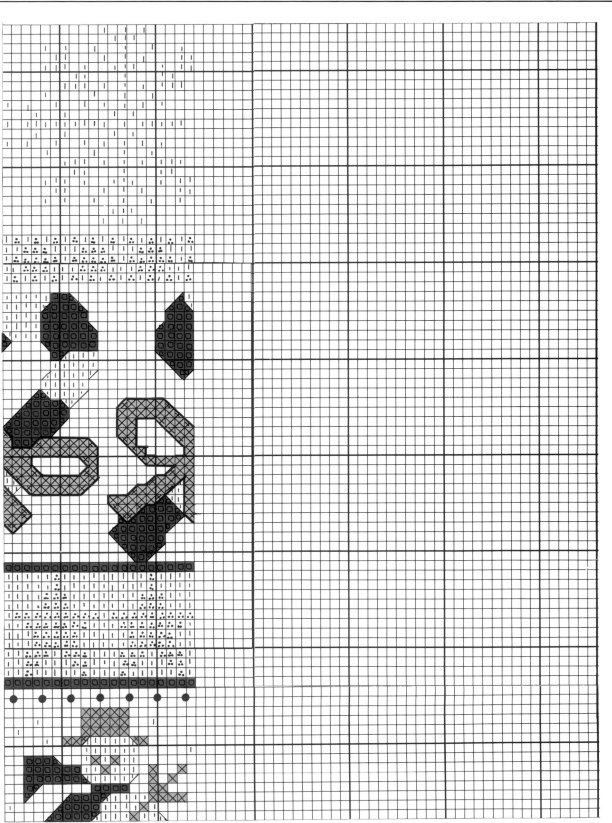

Sampler Stocking, top right

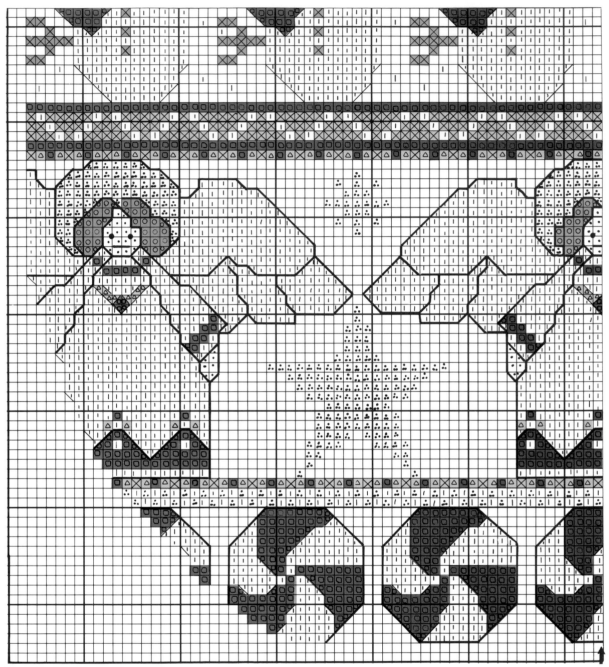

Sampler Stocking, bottom left

Sampler Stocking, bottom right

RED AND WHITE CHRISTMAS

Bright red-on-white
snowflake motifs lend
a touch of nineteenth century
Russian folk art to your home.
Create a fairy-tale setting for
your prettiest centerpiece with
the tasseled tablecloth.
Add Old World flair to
your Christmas decorations with
the bead-trimmed stocking
and ornaments.

TABLECLOTH

SAMPLE

Stitched on white Aida 14 over 1 and 2 threads, the finished design size for one repeat of the two border motifs is 6" x 3", not including the inner and outer rows of large cross-stitches. The fabric for the tablecloth was cut 45" x 45". The finished tablecloth is 35" square. The heavy black lines on the graph indicate repeats. Begin stitching first motif at one corner, placing first stitch (inside the heavy line at corner of graph) 3" from the edges. See the Placement Diagram before stitching repeats. Stitch first small snowflake according to graph, the remainder according to Placement Diagram. See Suppliers for specialty thread.

FABRICS	DESIGN SIZES
Aida 11	7¾" x 3⅞"
Aida 18	4¾" x 2⅜"
Hardanger 22	3¾" x 1⅞"

MATERIALS

- Completed cross-stitch; matching thread
- 2 packages of ⅜"-wide red rickrack; matching thread
- 4 balls of #666 red DMC Pearl Cotton
- 5" x 5" piece of cardboard

DIRECTIONS

1. Trim completed design piece ¾" from stitched outside border. Zigzag edges.

2. Using red thread, stitch rickrack to right side of design piece ¼" from zigzagged edge, beginning in one corner (see Diagram 1).

3. Turn edges of design piece under ⅝" along inner stitching line; pin. Using white thread, hem zigzagged edge.

4. To make one tassel, wind red pearl cotton around cardboard as many times as desired (see Diagram 2A). Tie bundle at top with strand of pearl cotton (see Diagram 2B). Cut strands opposite tie (see Diagram 2C).

5. Tightly wrap bundle with single strand of the pearl cotton (see Diagram 2D). Tie strand ends and push into tassel. Trim tassel to desired length. Repeat to make three more tassels.

6. Hand-sew one tassel to each corner of tablecloth (see photo).

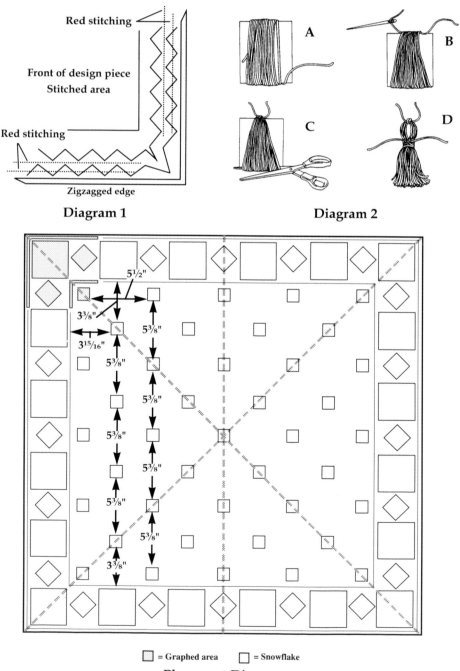

Red stitching
Front of design piece
Stitched area
Red stitching
Zigzagged edge

Diagram 1

A
B
C
D

Diagram 2

5½"
3⅜"
3¹⁵⁄₁₆"
5⅜"
5⅜"
5⅜"
5⅜"
5⅜"
5⅜"
5⅜"
3⅜"

▨ = Graphed area   ☐ = Snowflake

Placement Diagram

STOCKING

SAMPLE

Stitched on white Aida 14 over 1 and 2 threads, the finished design size for the stocking is 12" x 11¾". The fabric was cut 24" x 24". The finished design size for the stocking cuff is 9⅞" x 3⅝". The fabric was cut 29" x 12". See Suppliers for specialty thread.

Stocking

FABRICS	DESIGN SIZES
Aida 11	15¼" x 15"
Aida 18	9⅜" x 9⅛"
Hardanger 22	7⅝" x 7½"

Stocking Cuff

FABRICS	DESIGN SIZES
Aida 11	12½" x 4½"
Aida 18	7⅝" x 2¾"
Hardanger 22	6¼" x 2¼"

MATERIALS

- 2 completed cross-stitch pieces; matching thread
- Dressmaker's pen
- ½ yard of unstitched white Aida 14
- 5 yards of ⅜"-wide red rickrack; matching thread
- 5 yards of ¼"-diameter red corded piping
- 1 yard of cotton white fabric
- 6½" length of 1"-wide red ribbon
- 6 skeins of red DMC Floralia Wool #7891
- 5" x 5" piece of cardboard
- Large-eyed needle
- 4 red wooden beads

DIRECTIONS

All seams are ¼".

1. With design centered, trim completed cuff design piece to 19¼" x 4¼". Using design piece as pattern, cut matching piece from unstitched Aida 14 for cuff lining.

2. From rickrack and corded piping, cut two 19¼" lengths. Refer to photo to see how piping and rickrack align. Pin one length of piping over one length of rickrack on right side of each long edge of cuff design piece (see Diagram 1 on page 31). Stitch. With right sides together, stitch short ends of cuff; do not turn.

3. With right sides together, stitch short edges of cuff lining; turn right side out. Aligning seams, slide lining inside design piece. Stitch top edge of lining to design piece along stitching line of trim. Draw lining up out of design piece and down, so bottom edges align (see Diagram 2 on page 31). Turn cuff; press with lining on inside.

4. To complete cuff, turn in raw edges of lining and cuff; slipstitch in place. Set aside.

5. Make stocking pattern on page 32. Transfer to completed stocking design piece with design centered horizontally and top edge of stitched area 4½" below top of stocking. Cut out stocking. From unstitched Aida 14, cut one stocking back. From white fabric, cut two stockings for lining.

6. Stitch rickrack and corded piping to right side of stocking design piece as in Step 2. With right sides together, stitch design piece to stocking back along stitching line of trim, leaving top open. Turn.

7. To make hanger, make loop with ribbon, and, with raw edges aligned, baste to top of stocking back near heel seam.

8. To make stocking lining, stitch lining pieces with right sides together, leaving open at top and for 3" along seam above heel; do not turn. Slide lining over stocking, aligning top edges and seams. Stitch around stocking top. Pull stocking through opening in lining, turning right side out. Slipstitch opening closed. Tuck lining inside stocking.

9. Slide cuff over stocking so rickrack at top edge is ¼" above stocking top. Hand-sew cuff to stocking, securing hanger.

10. To make one tassel, use 3 skeins of red Floralia Wool, reserving two 14" lengths. Use one length to wrap tassel (see Steps 4-5 and Diagrams 3A–3D on page 92). Make two tassels.

11. Thread needle with remaining 14" length of Floralia Wool. Draw each thread end through the top of the tassel, then through two red wooden beads. Use needle to insert one thread end at a time through stocking cuff near top and at heel seam. Knot and trim the ends. Repeat to finish and attach second tassel.

ORNAMENTS

SAMPLE
All three ornaments are stitched on white Aida 14 over 1 and 2 threads. The finished design size for each ornament is 3" x 3". The fabric was cut 8" x 8" for each. The motifs are taken from the Stocking Cuff on page 93 and use the same code.

Three Ornaments

FABRICS	DESIGN SIZES
Aida 11	3⅞" x 3⅞"
Aida 18	2⅜" x 2⅜"
Hardanger 22	1⅞" x 1⅞"

One Ornament • Stitch Count: 42 x 42

MATERIALS FOR ONE

- Completed cross-stitch; matching thread
- 4" x 4" piece of un-stitched Aida 14
- ½ yard of ⅜"-wide red rickrack, ½"-wide red loop braid or ⅜"-wide red piping; matching thread
- Polyester stuffing
- ¾ yard of ½"-wide red satin ribbon
- 4-8 assorted red wooden beads

DIRECTIONS
All seams are 1/4".

1. Trim completed design piece to 4" x 4". Zigzag edges.

2. Stitch desired trim to design piece on right side, ³⁄₁₆" from zigzagged edge (see Diagram).

3. With right sides together, stitch 4" x 4" piece of unstitched Aida 14 to design piece along stitching line of trim, leaving one edge open.

4. Turn. Stuff moderately. Slipstitch opening closed.

5. From ribbon, cut one 18" length. Make bow; notch ends. Make loop with remaining ribbon. Cross ends. Center behind bow. Tack bow and loop to one corner of ornament front (see photo).

6. String bead groups as desired on red thread. Tack to corners or bottom of ornament.

Table cloth ★

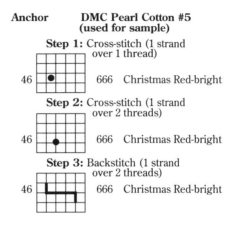

Anchor		DMC Pearl Cotton #5 (used for sample)
	Step 1:	Cross-stitch (1 strand over 1 thread)
46		666 Christmas Red-bright
	Step 2:	Cross-stitch (1 strand over 2 threads)
46		666 Christmas Red-bright
	Step 3:	Backstitch (1 strand over 2 threads)
46		666 Christmas Red-bright

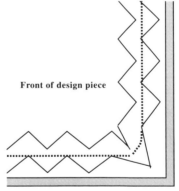

Front of design piece

Zigzagged edge

Diagram

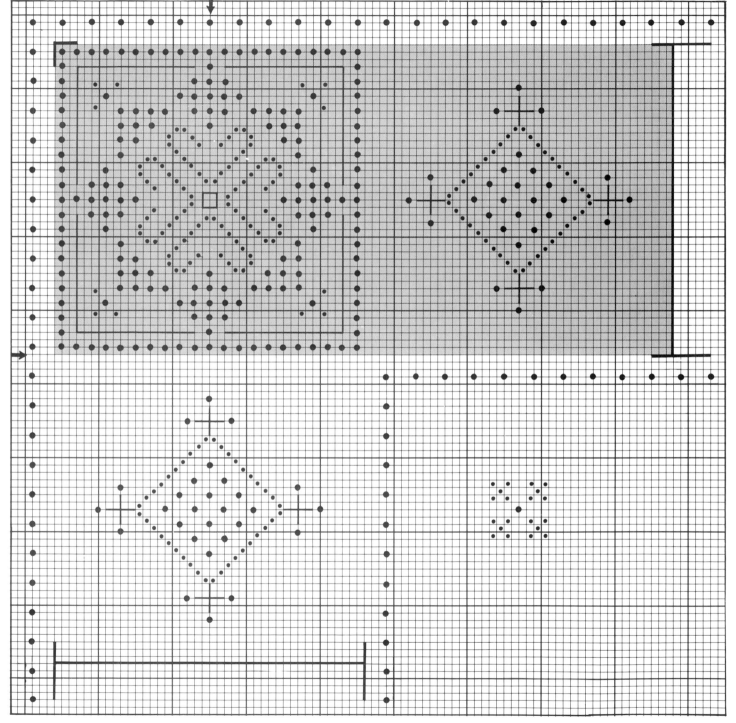

**Tablecloth Border Motif • Stitch Count: 86 x 42
for one Repeat of Two Border Motifs**

RED AND WHITE CHRISTMAS

Stocking and Cuff ★

**DMC Floralia Wool
(used for sample)**

Step 1: Cross-stitch (1 strand over 1 thread)

7891   Red

Step 2: Cross-stitch (1 strand over 2 threads)

7891   Red

Step 3: Backstitch (1 strand over 2 threads)

7891   Red

Stocking Cuff, left • Stitch Count: 138 x 50

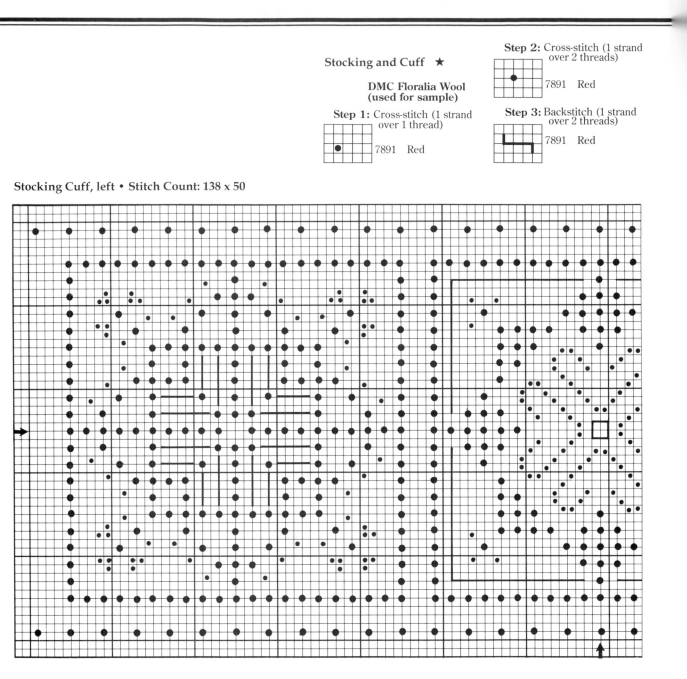

Stocking, top left • Stitch Count: 168 x 165

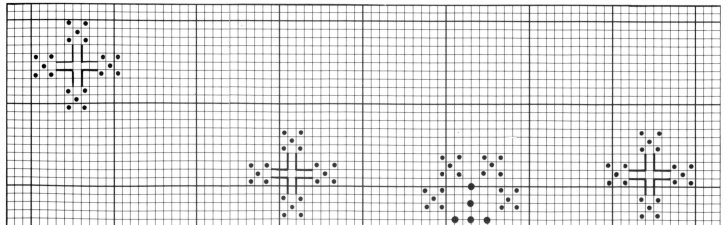

Stocking Cuff, right

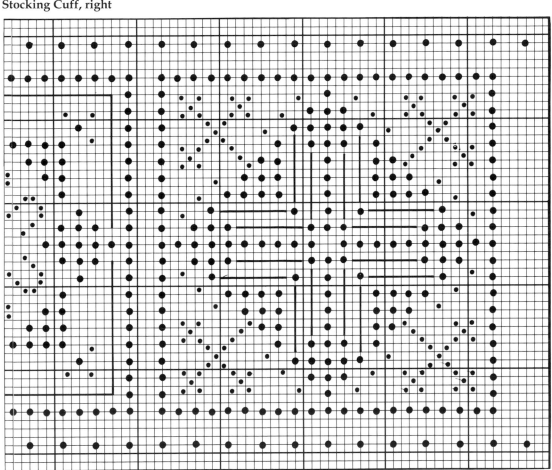

Stocking, top right

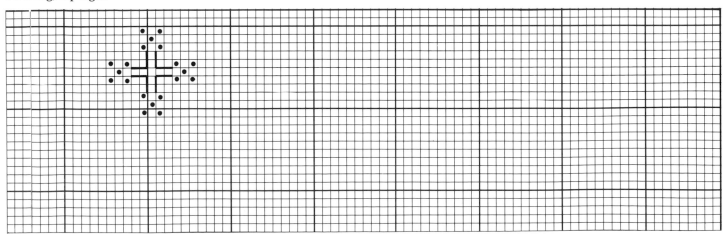

Stocking, left center

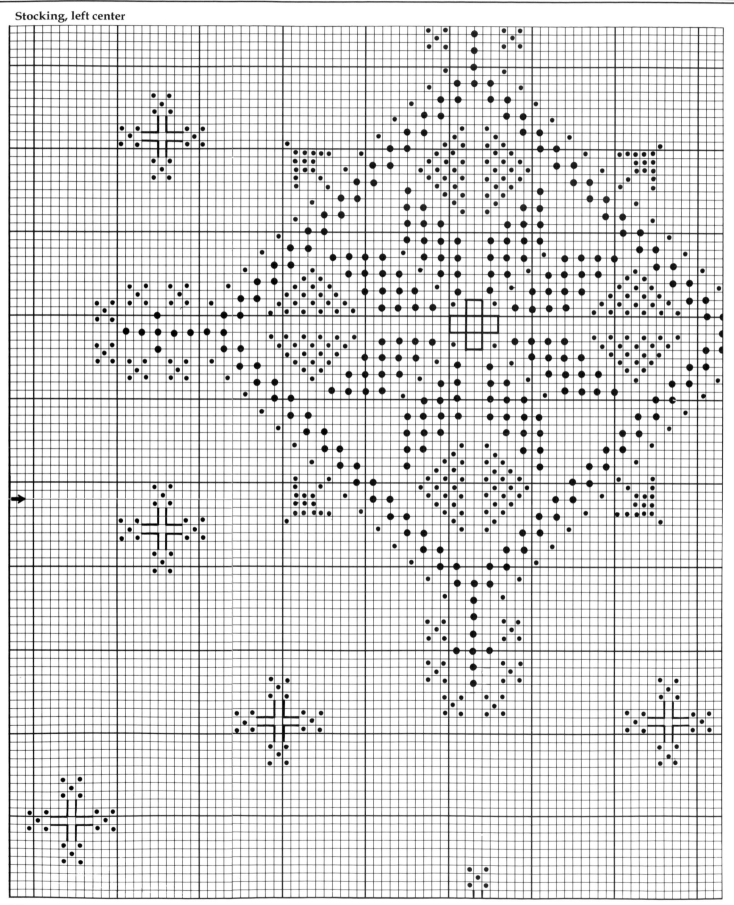

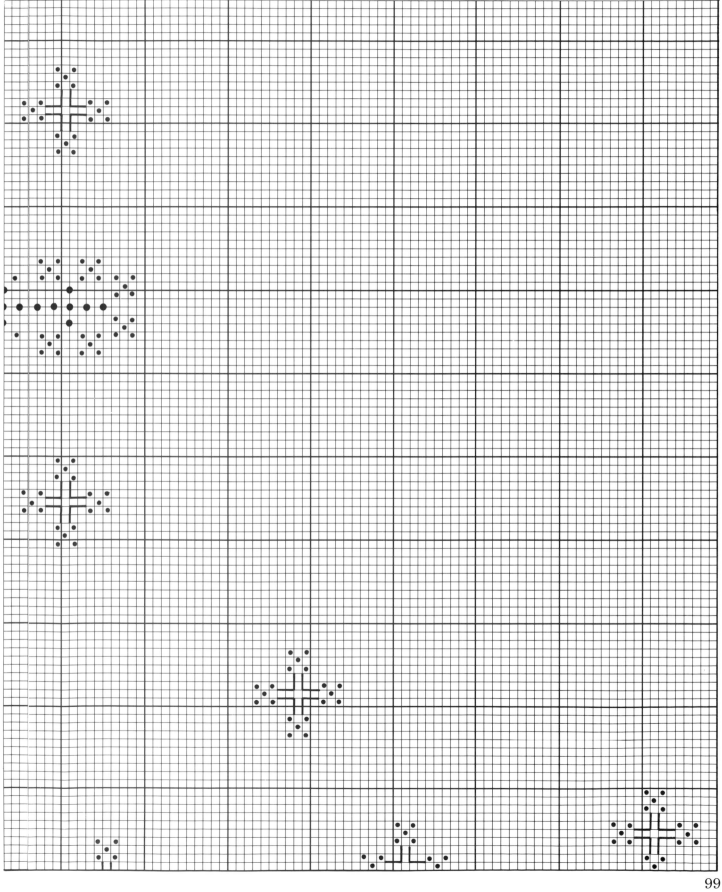

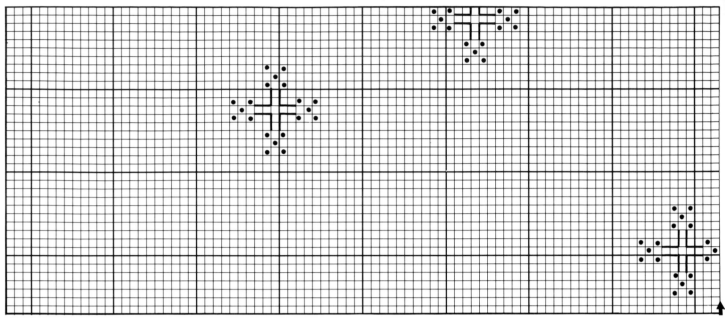

Stocking, bottom left

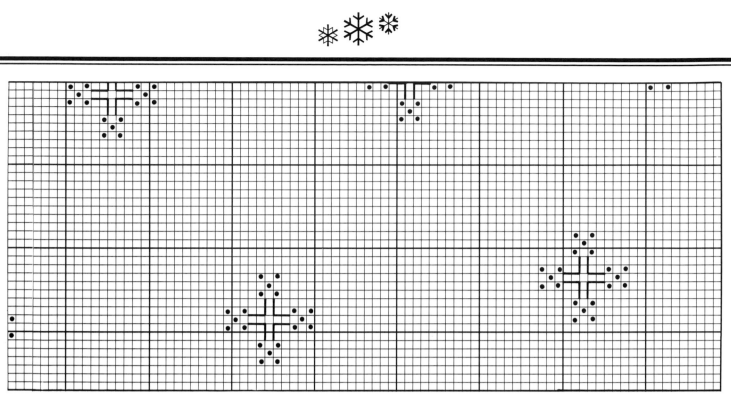

Stocking, bottom right

HOLIDAY HERBS

Fragrant herbs impart savory smells
to a busy holiday kitchen.
Keep bouquets of fresh herbs
nearby throughout the Christmas
season and use them as inspiration
to stitch this pretty apron, towel
and wreath. Then decorate
the festive table with
the matching place mats
and napkins to complete
the long-awaited feast!

APRON

SAMPLE

Stitched on ivory Aida 14 over 1 and 2 threads, the finished design size for the apron top is 6⅞" x 11⅝". The fabric was cut 27" x 35". The heavy black lines on the graph indicate repeats for completing the checkerboard border at the bottom of the apron. See Step 1 of the directions before beginning to stitch.

Apron Top

FABRICS	DESIGN SIZES
Aida 11	8¾" x 14⅞"
Aida 18	5⅜" x 9"
Hardanger	4⅜" x 7⅜"

MATERIALS

- Completed cross-stitch
- Dressmaker's pen
- ⅜ yard of dark blue fabric; matching thread
- 1 yard of ivory cotton fabric for lining

DIRECTIONS

1. Before stitching design, make apron pattern. Using dressmaker's pen, transfer pattern to Aida 14; do not cut out. Begin stitching border top with top edge of checkerboard centered ½" below top edge of bib. Begin stitching bottom border with bottom edge of checkerboard centered ¼" above bottom edge of apron; stitch to fill. When stitching is completed, cut out apron.

2. Place ivory fabric wrong side up on flat surface. Center apron right side up on fabric; baste together. Trim ivory fabric to match raw apron edges.

3. From dark blue fabric, cut 2¾"-wide bias strips, piecing as needed to make 4 yards of binding. Fold binding in half lengthwise; press. Cut into one 8" length, one 54" length and one 77" length.

4. Align raw edges of 8" binding with top edge of apron bib on wrong side; stitch ¼" from top edges. Fold binding over apron edge to front of apron; topstitch (see Diagram 1). In same manner, bind side and bottom apron edges with 54" binding, mitering corners.

5. Refer to Diagram 2 to bind armholes and make ties from remaining binding. Leaving about 28" free at each end, attach binding as in Step 4. Press under raw edge of ties and neck strap as shown in Diagram 3, and topstitch binding from end to end. Knot ends.

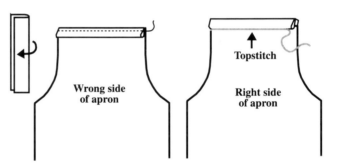

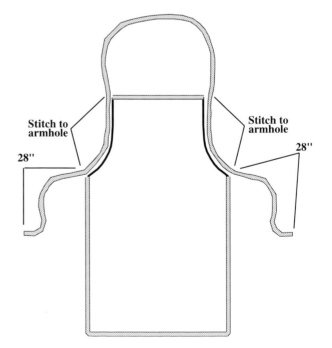

Diagram 1

Wrong side of apron

Topstitch

Right side of apron

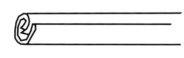

Diagram 3

Diagram 2

Stitch to armhole

Stitch to armhole

28"

28"

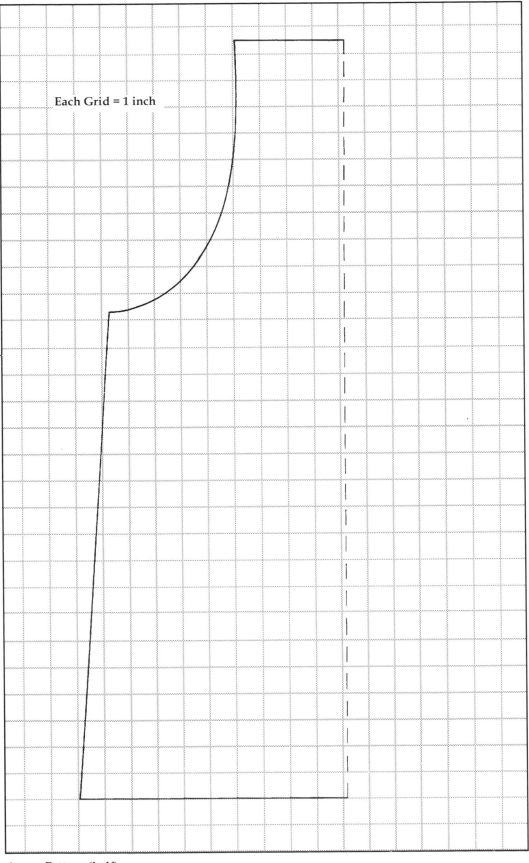

Each Grid = 1 inch

Apron Pattern (half)

PLACE MAT

SAMPLE
Stitched on oatmeal Almeria 22 over 2 threads, the finished design size is 4⅛" x 11½". The fabric was cut 23" x 17". Begin stitching design with left edge of checkerboard border parallel to and 3" from left short edge of fabric.

FABRICS	DESIGN SIZES
Aida 14	3¼" x 9"
Aida 18	2½" x 7"
Hardanger 22	2⅛" x 5¾"

MATERIALS

- Completed cross-stitch
- 18½" x 12½" piece of unstitched oatmeal Almeria 22
- ¼ yard of dark blue fabric; matching thread

DIRECTIONS

1. With completed design vertically centered and left edge of checkerboard border 1" from left edge of measurement, trim the fabric to 18½" x 12½". Zigzag fabric edges.

2. To make place mat back, zigzag edges of unstitched oatmeal Almeria 22. With wrong sides together, baste design piece and back together.

3. From dark blue fabric, cut 2¾"-wide bias strips, piecing as needed to make 1¾ yards of binding. Fold binding in half lengthwise; press. With raw edges aligned and using ¼" seam allowance, bind edges of place mat; begin in middle of one edge, miter corners and join ends neatly.

4. Fold binding over edge of place mat; hand-sew.

NAPKIN

SAMPLE
Stitched on oatmeal Almeria 22 over 2 threads, the napkin border motif is taken from the Place Mat on pages 107-108. The fabric was cut 16½" x 16½" for one napkin. Stitch border with the outside edges 1" from the fabric edges. Finished napkin is 15½ " x 15½".

MATERIALS

- Completed cross-stitch; matching thread

DIRECTIONS

1. With design centered, trim fabric to 16½" x 16½". Zigzag fabric edges, then fold edges ¼" twice to wrong side all around, mitering corners. Pin and press.

2. Stitch napkin hem.

TOWEL

SAMPLE
Stitched on Blue Mist Check Café Cross-stitch Towel over 1, the finished design size is 3⅜" x 2⅞". See Suppliers for specialty towel.

FABRICS	DESIGN SIZES
Aida 11	4⅜" x 3⅝"
Aida 14	3⅜" x 2⅞"
Aida 18	2⅝" x 2¼"
Hardanger 22	2⅛" x 1⅞"

WREATH

SAMPLE
Stitched on oatmeal Almeria 22 over 2, the finished design size is 12½" x 12½". The fabric was cut 19" x 19".

FABRICS	DESIGN SIZES
Aida 11	12½" x 12½"
Aida 14	9⅞" x 9⅞"
Aida 18	7⅝" x 7⅝"
Hardanger 22	6¼" x 6¼"

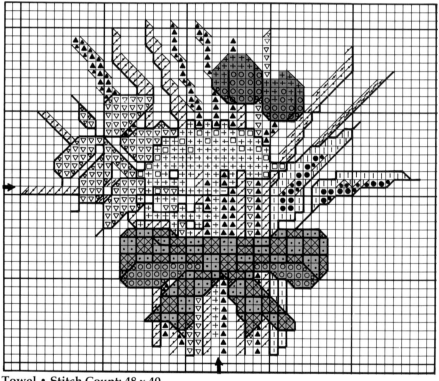

Towel • Stitch Count: 48 x 40

★★ DMC   Anchor (used for sample)

Step 1: Cross-stitch (2 strands)

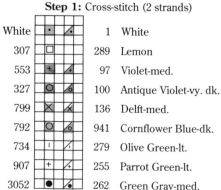

	DMC	Anchor	
White		1	White
307		289	Lemon
553		97	Violet-med.
327		100	Antique Violet-vy. dk.
799		136	Delft-med.
792		941	Cornflower Blue-dk.
734		279	Olive Green-lt.
907		255	Parrot Green-lt.
3052		262	Green Gray-med.

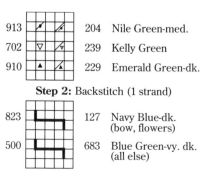

	DMC	Anchor	
913		204	Nile Green-med.
702		239	Kelly Green
910		229	Emerald Green-dk.

Step 2: Backstitch (1 strand)

	DMC	Anchor	
823		127	Navy Blue-dk. (bow, flowers)
500		683	Blue Green-vy. dk. (all else)

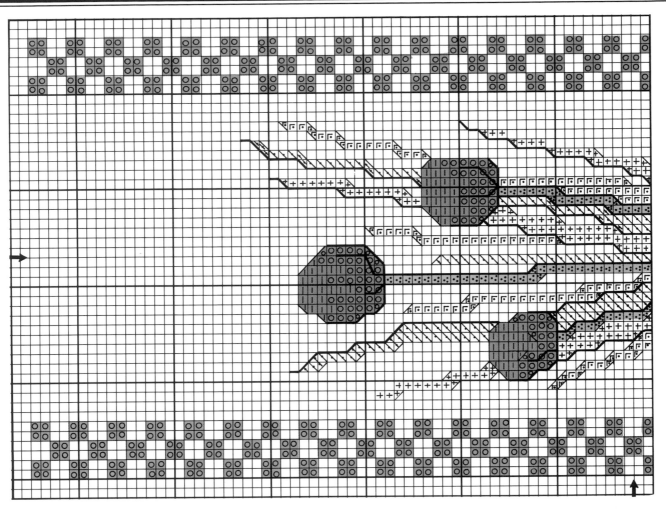

Place Mat, top • Stitch Count: 46 x 126

★★ DMC   Anchor (used for sample)

Step 1: Cross-stitch (2 strands)

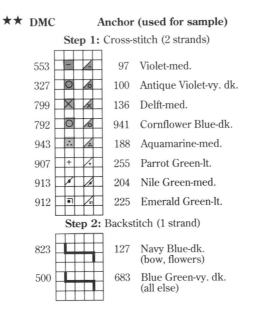

553			97	Violet-med.
327			100	Antique Violet-vy. dk.
799			136	Delft-med.
792			941	Cornflower Blue-dk.
943			188	Aquamarine-med.
907			255	Parrot Green-lt.
913			204	Nile Green-med.
912			225	Emerald Green-lt.

Step 2: Backstitch (1 strand)

| 823 | | | 127 | Navy Blue-dk. (bow, flowers) |
| 500 | | | 683 | Blue Green-vy. dk. (all else) |

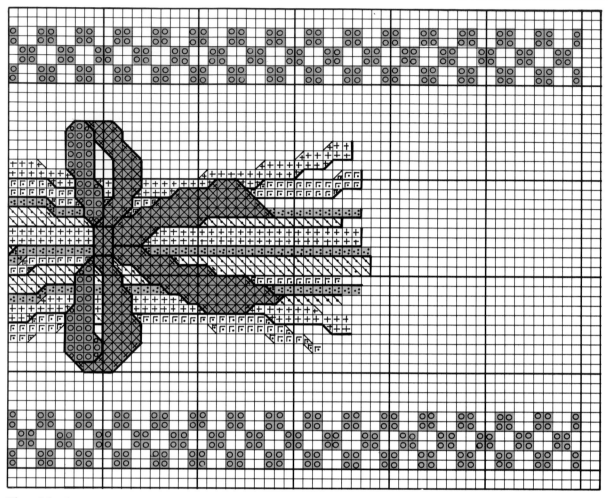

Place Mat, bottom

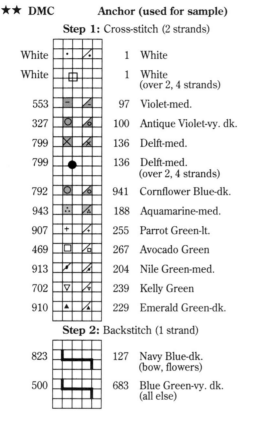

★★ **DMC**   **Anchor (used for sample)**

Step 1: Cross-stitch (2 strands)

White		1 White
White		1 White (over 2, 4 strands)
553		97 Violet-med.
327		100 Antique Violet-vy. dk.
799		136 Delft-med.
799		136 Delft-med. (over 2, 4 strands)
792		941 Cornflower Blue-dk.
943		188 Aquamarine-med.
907		255 Parrot Green-lt.
469		267 Avocado Green
913		204 Nile Green-med.
702		239 Kelly Green
910		229 Emerald Green-dk.

Step 2: Backstitch (1 strand)

823		127 Navy Blue-dk. (bow, flowers)
500		683 Blue Green-vy. dk. (all else)

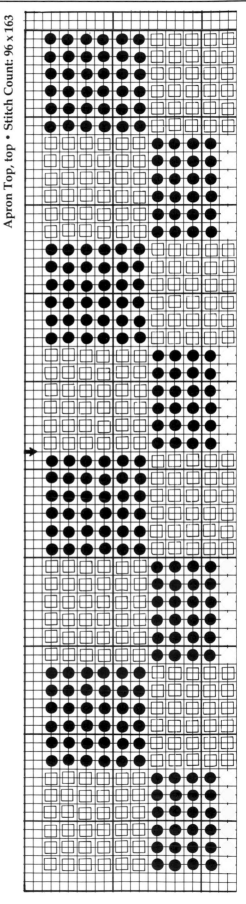

Apron Top, top • Stitch Count: 96 x 163

Apron Top, center

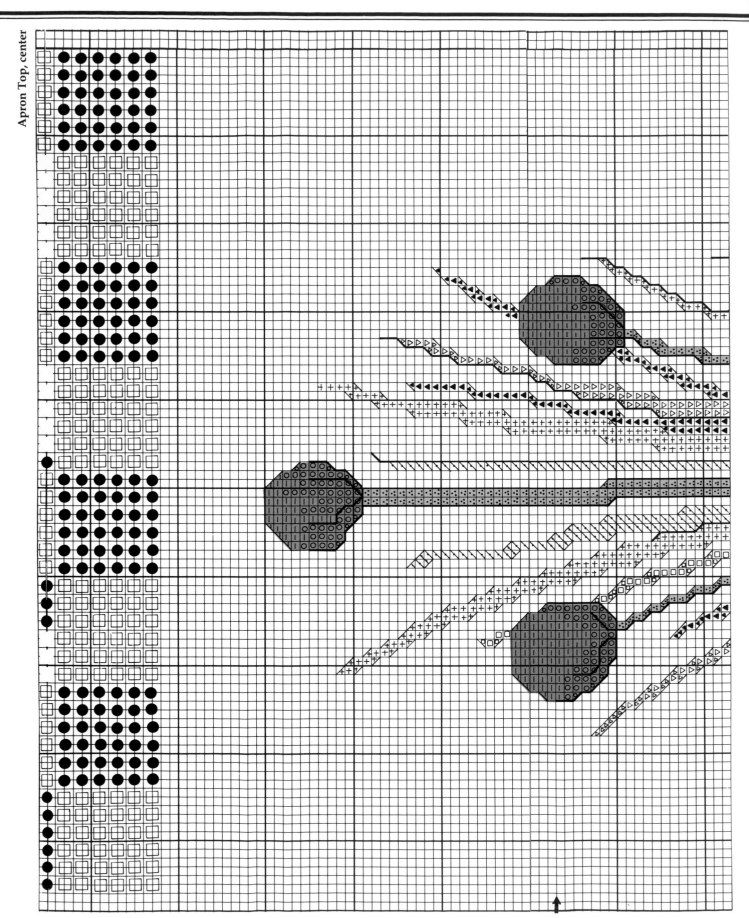

Apron Top, bottom

HOLIDAY HERBS

★★ DMC   Anchor (used for sample)

Step 1: Cross-stitch (2 strands)

White	1	White
444	290	Lemon-dk.
553	97	Violet-med.
327	100	Antique Violet-vy. dk.
799	136	Delft-med.
792	941	Cornflower Blue-dk.
943	188	Aquamarine-med.

734	279	Olive Green-lt.
732	281	Olive Green
907	255	Parrot Green-lt.
469	267	Avocado Green
937	268	Avocado Green-med.
3052	262	Green Gray-med.
913	204	Nile Green-med.
702	239	Kelly Green
910	229	Emerald Green-dk.

503	875	Blue Green-med.
502	877	Blue Green
500	683	Blue Green-vy. dk.

Step 2: Backstitch (1 strand)

823	127	Navy Blue-dk. (bow, flowers)
500	683	Blue Green-vy. dk. (all else)

Wreath, top left • Stitch Count: 138 x 138

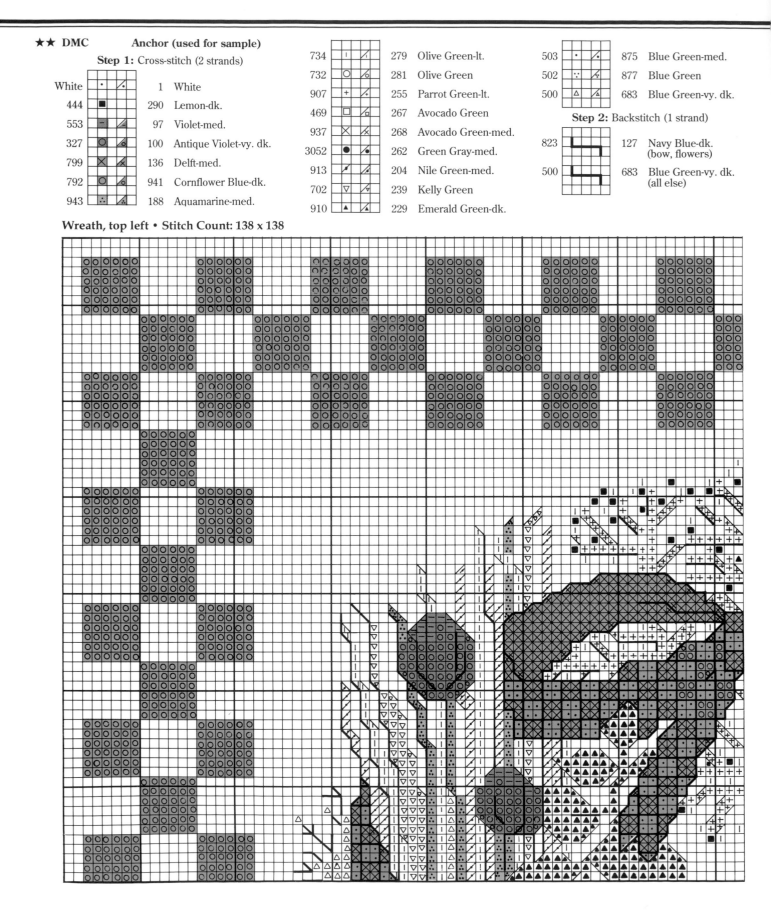

112

Wreath, top right

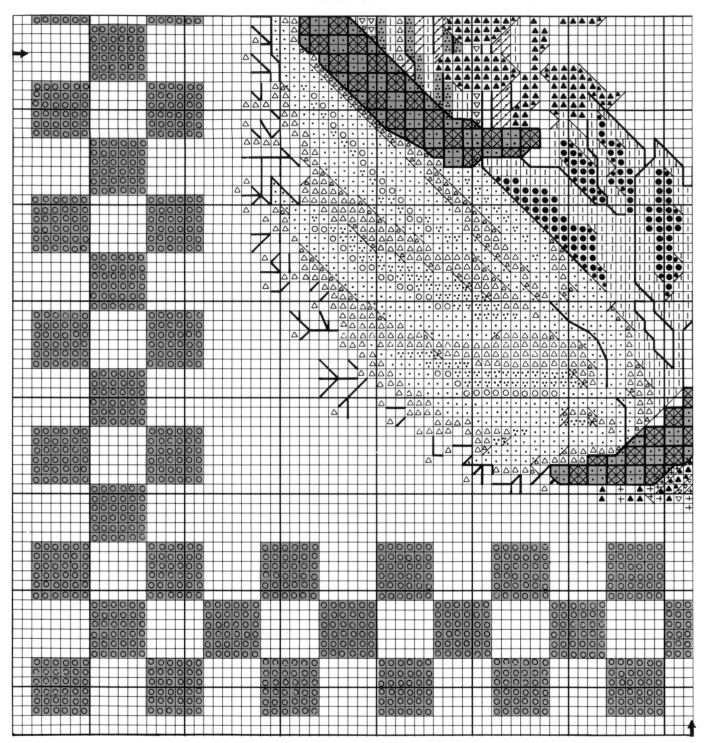

Wreath, bottom left

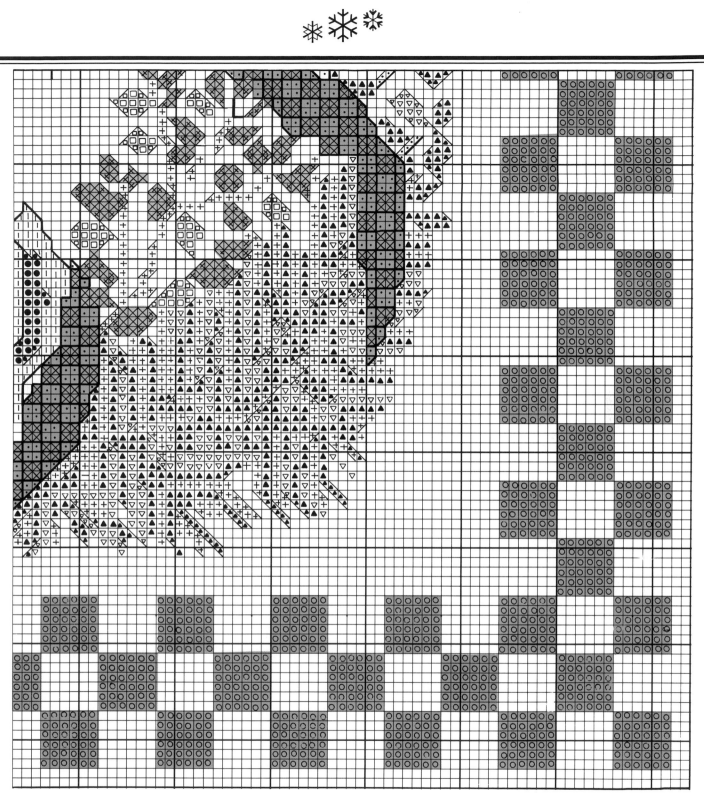

Wreath, bottom right

SANTA AND MRS. SANTA

Invite the season's most popular
and beloved couple into your home
this Christmas! They will be happy
to keep a twinkling eye on
good little boys and girls of all ages.
These perky, huggable stuffed dolls,
so easy to create, are perfect
for giving or keeping.

DOLLS

SANTA SAMPLE
Stitched on red Aida 11 over 1, the finished design size is 9⅛" x 12½". The fabric was cut 13" x 17".

FABRICS	DESIGN SIZES
Aida 14	7⅛" x 9¾"
Aida 18	5½" x 7⅝"
Hardanger 22	4½" x 6¼"

MRS. SANTA SAMPLE
Stitched on red Aida 11 over 1, the finished design size is 9⅛" x 11¼". The fabric was cut 13" x 16".

FABRICS	DESIGN SIZES
Aida 14	7⅛" x 8⅞"
Aida 18	5½" x 6⅞"
Hardanger 22	4½" x 5⅝"

MATERIALS FOR ONE

- Completed cross-stitch; matching thread
- Dressmaker's pen
- 13" x 17" piece of un-stitched red Aida 11
- 4½" x 7½" piece of mat board
- Polyester stuffing
- 3"-long white rayon tassel (for Mrs. Santa Claus)

DIRECTIONS

All seams are ¼".

1. Trim completed design piece according to heavy black outline on graph. Using design piece as pattern, cut one doll back from unstitched Aida 11.

2. Make gusset pattern. Cut one gusset from mat board and one from Aida 11.

3. With right sides together, stitch design piece to doll back, leaving bottom open. Do not turn.

4. With right sides together, stitch fabric gusset to bottom edge of doll, leaving a large opening. Turn doll right side out.

5. Begin stuffing doll firmly from head down. Stop just above gusset. Insert mat board gusset through opening and position flat over fabric gusset.

6. Finish stuffing doll, making sure mat board gusset remains flat and doll is stuffed firmly enough to stand upright.

7. Slipstitch opening closed. Tack tassel to peak of cap on Mrs. Santa Claus Doll (see photo).

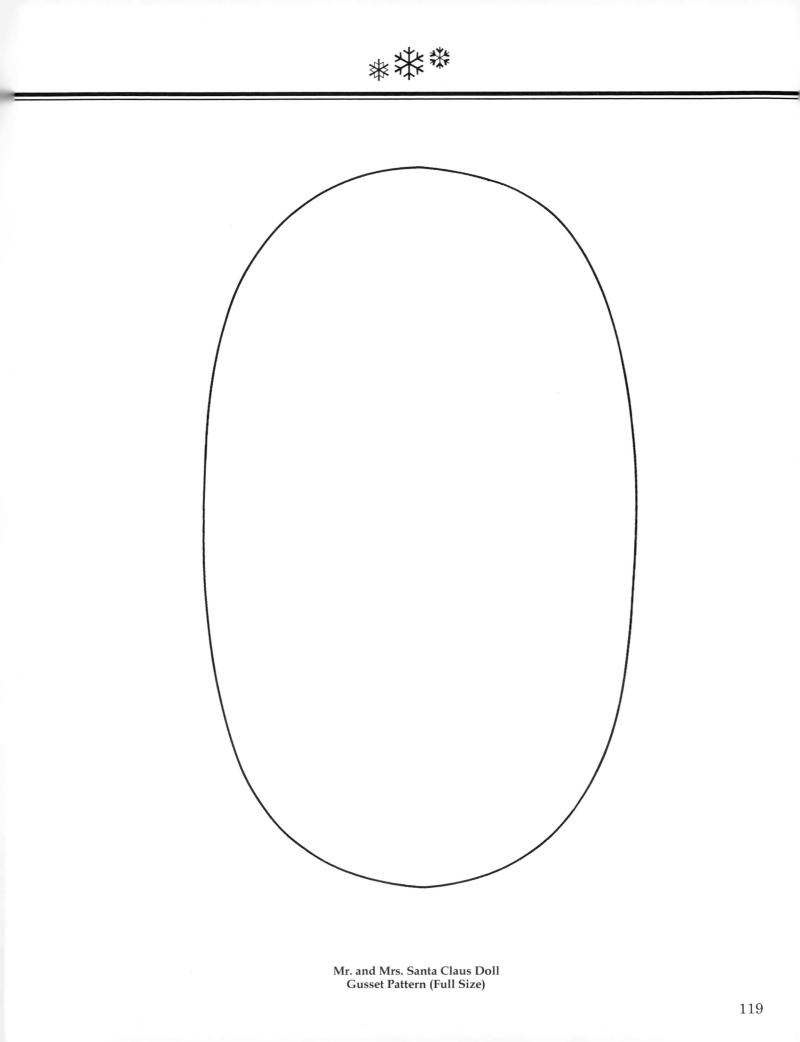

Mr. and Mrs. Santa Claus Doll
Gusset Pattern (Full Size)

★ **Anchor**   **DMC (used for sample)**

Step 1: Cross-stitch (3strands)

1	White
50	3716	Wild Rose-lt.
42	335	Rose
78	601	Cranberry-dk.
44	814	Garnet-dk.
229	700	Christmas Green-bright
		DMC Lt. Gold Fil Or Clair (2 strands)
403	310	Black

Step 2: Backstitch (1 strand)

| 403 | 310 | Black |

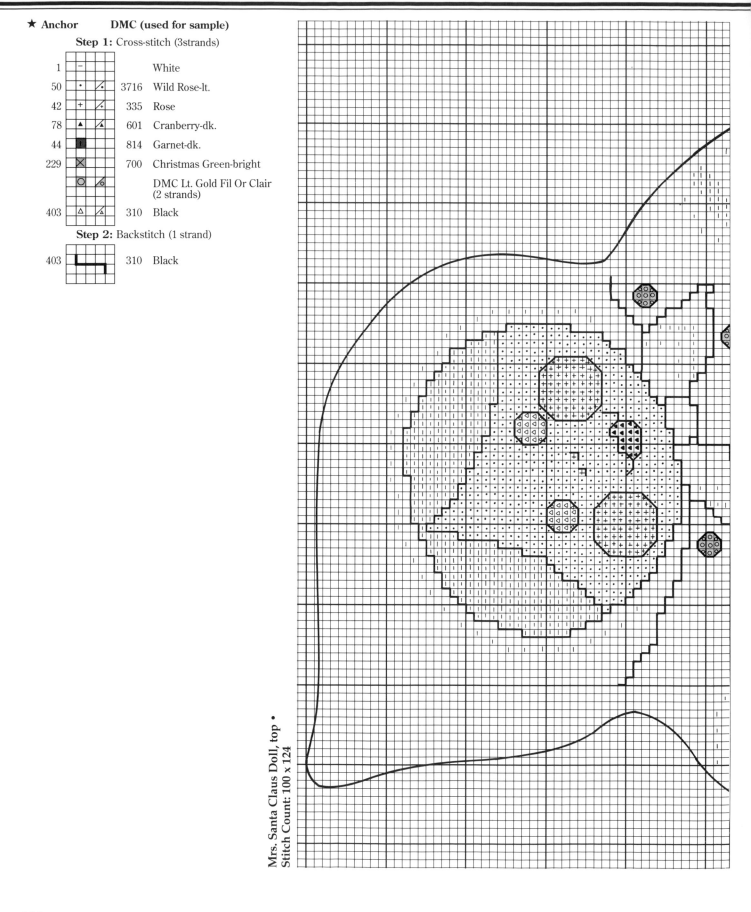

Mrs. Santa Claus Doll, top •
Stitch Count: 100 x 124

Mrs. Santa Claus Doll, bottom

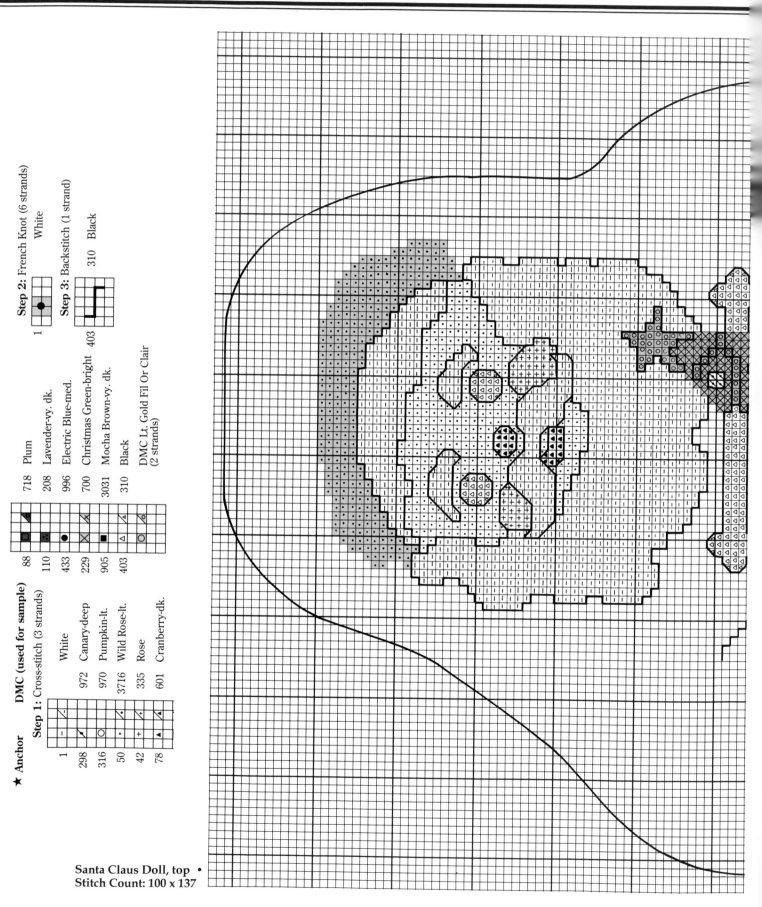

★ Anchor

DMC (used for sample)

Step 1: Cross-stitch (3 strands)

1		White
298		972 Canary-deep
316		970 Pumpkin-lt.
50		3716 Wild Rose-lt.
42		335 Rose
78		601 Cranberry-dk.
88		718 Plum
110		208 Lavender-vy. dk.
433		996 Electric Blue-med.
229		700 Christmas Green-bright
905		3031 Mocha Brown-vy. dk.
403		310 Black
		DMC Lt. Gold Fil Or Clair (2 strands)

Step 2: French Knot (6 strands)

1	White

Step 3: Backstitch (1 strand)

	310 Black
	403

Santa Claus Doll, top •
Stitch Count: 100 x 137

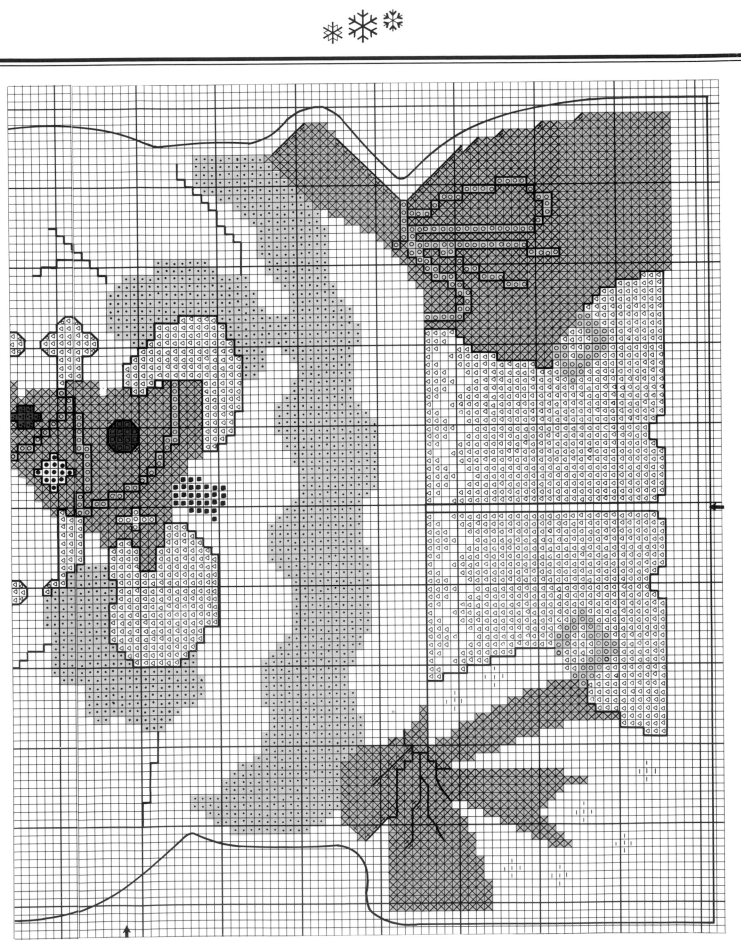

Santa Claus Doll, bottom

GENERAL INSTRUCTIONS

CROSS-STITCHING

EASY REFERENCE FEATURES

The SAMPLE paragraphs describe the design pieces in each photograph. They also contain any special instructions for stitching or for cutting fabric. When applicable, finished design sizes are also given for other fabrics you may wish to use.

On the graphs, each square containing a symbol represents one cross-stitch and corresponds to a specific thread color as indicated on the color code. The stitch count printed with a graph lists first the width, then the length of the design. Projects that do not have their own graphs have stitch counts shown below the SAMPLE paragraph where applicable.

The color codes identify thread by color, number, and brand. The symbols correspond to the symbols on the graphs. The color codes also indicate the kinds of stitches and number of floss strands to use.

FABRICS

The designs in this book are worked on even-weave fabrics made especially for cross-stitching. The number of threads-per-inch determines the finished design size.

PREPARING THE FABRIC

Cut fabric at least 3" larger on all sides than the design size, or as specified in the SAMPLE paragraph. To prevent fraying, whipstitch or zigzag raw fabric edges before stitching. Using a stretcher bar frame or a hoop keeps fabric from wrinkling, ensuring uniform stitches.

PERFORATED PAPER AND PERFORATED PLASTIC

Cut perforated paper or plastic at least 1" larger on all sides than the finished design size. Stitch over one space. Do not pull thread too tight; the small spaces between the perforations may tear. When trimming the completed work, trim to one hole outside the design. Do not cut into any hole holding a stitch. Work done on perforated plastic may be cleaned with cold water; do not iron or dry clean.

CENTERING THE DESIGN

Unless otherwise indicated in the directions, the design should be centered on the fabric. Fold fabric in half horizontally, then vertically. Place a pin in the point of the fold to mark the center. Locate the center of the design on the graph by following the paths of the vertical and horizontal arrows printed on the edges of each graph to their intersection. Begin stitching at the center of the graph and fabric.

NEEDLES

A blunt tapestry needle, size 24 or 26, will slip easily through fabric holes without piercing fabric threads. Never leave a needle in the design area of the work; it may leave rust or a permanent impression on the fabric.

FLOSS

Cut thread into 18" lengths; longer pieces tend to twist and knot. Run floss over a damp sponge to straighten. Separate the strands, then use the number of strands indicated in the color code. Thread should lie flat; if it begins to twist, suspend the needle and allow it to unwind.

Secure the thread by inserting the needle up from the underside of the fabric at the starting point. Hold 1" of thread behind the fabric and stitch over it with the first few stitches. Another method for securing thread is the waste knot. Knot the thread and bring the needle down through the fabric about 1" from where first stitch will be. Work several stitches over the thread to secure. Cut off the knot later. To finish thread, run it under several stitches on the back of the work.

To carry thread, weave it under previously worked stitches on the back of the design. Do not carry thread across fabric that is not or will not be stitched. Loose threads, especially dark ones, will show through.

CLEANING COMPLETED WORK

Soak finished design piece in cold water with mild soap for 5-10 minutes; rinse. Roll in a towel to remove excess water; do not wring. Place face down on a dry towel and iron on a warm setting until dry.

BEADWORK

Cross-stitch all non-beaded areas of design before doing any beadwork. Apply each bead in the same manner as a cross-stitch: stitch from lower left to upper right, passing floss through bead; bring needle up again at lower right, pass through bead again, and insert at upper left. When working in rows, first make all left-to-right diagonal stitches in the row, then return to secure beads with the right-to-left diagonal stitches.

STITCHES USED

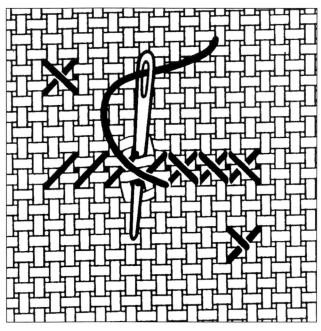

Cross-Stitch and Half-Cross Stitch Diagram

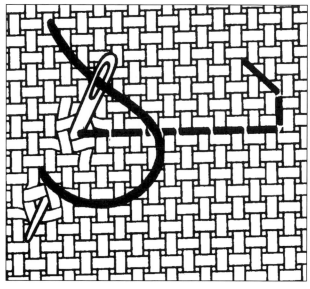

Backstitch Diagram

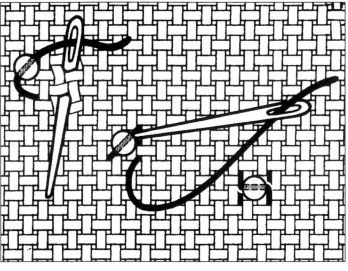

Beading Diagram

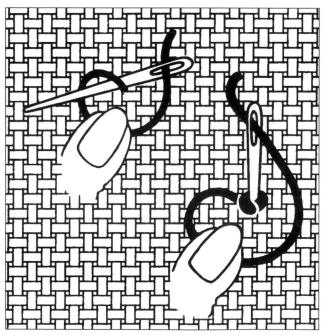

French Knot Diagram

GENERAL INSTRUCTIONS

PATTERNS

Use tracing paper or Mylar to trace patterns. All patterns in this book include a ¼" seam allowance unless otherwise specified. Patterns too large for the page are reduced and printed on a grid. Each grid square equals 1". To enlarge the pattern, mark grid lines 1" apart on a large sheet of paper, filling the paper. Begin marking dots on the grid lines where the reduced pattern intersects the corresponding line. Connect the dots. You may also purchase preprinted 1" graph paper.

To use half patterns, fold fabric, then place dashed line on pattern on fold and cut out pattern.

CORDED PIPING

With wrong sides together and raw edges aligned, fold the pieced bias strip in half lengthwise with the cording in the fold. Stitch the fabric close to the cording.

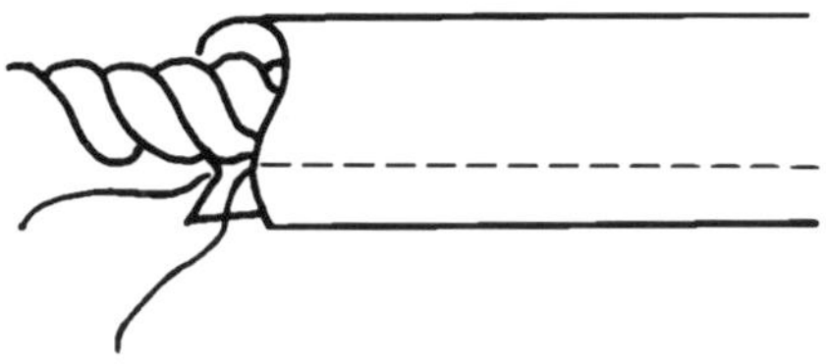

MITERING CORNERS

Sew border strips of fabric up to but not through the seam allowance (see Diagram). Backstitch. Repeat at all four corners. Fold two adjacent border strips or fabric corners together as shown in the Diagram. Mark, then sew at a 45-degree angle. Trim seam allowance to ¼".

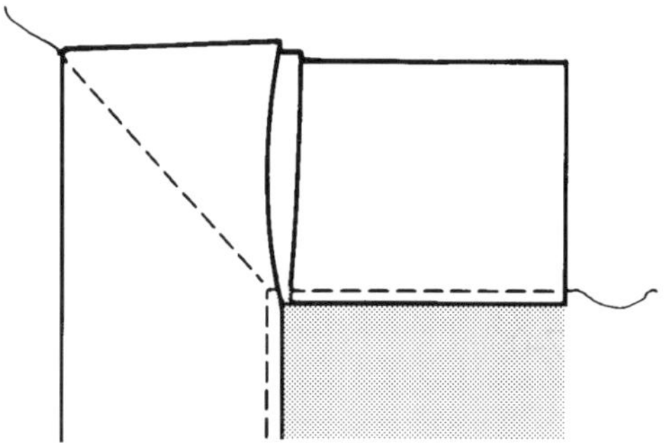

Corded Piping Diagram

Mitering Corners Diagram

SUPPLIERS

To find out where you can purchase or order supplies, contact the following:

Zweigart/Joan Toggitt Ltd.
Weston Canal Plaza
2 Riverview Drive
Somerset, NJ 08873
(908) 271-1949

Cream, white, ivory Aida 14
White Country Aida 7
Red, navy, white Aida 11
Raw Linen 25
Cream Gloria 14 Afghan Fabric
Oatmeal Almeria 22
Dirty linen Dublin Linen 25

Charles Craft
P.O. Box 1049
Laurinburg, NC 28353
(800) 277-0980

Black Aida 18
Café Cross-Stitch Towel
Delft blue, black Aida 14

Darice Incorporated
21160 Drake Road
Strongsville, OH 44136
(800) 321-1491

White Perforated Plastic 14

The DMC Corporation
Contact:
American Needlewoman
1-800-433-2231
Herrschner's
1-800-441-0838

DMC Floss
Fil Or Clair floss
Fil Argent Clair floss
Medici Floss
DMC Pearl Cotton
Floralia Wool

Gay Bowles Sales, Inc.
P.O. Box 1060
Janesville WI, 53547
(608) 754-9466

Mill Hill Beads

Kreinik Mfg. Co, Inc.
P.O. Box 1966
Parkersburg, WV 26101
(800) 537-2166

#8 Braid 002 Gold
#8 Braid 001 Silver

Reed Baxter Woodcrafts Inc.
P.O. Box 2186
Eugene, OR 97402
(503) 683-1210

Wooden box

Coats & Clark
30 Patewood Drive, Suite 351
Greenville, SC 29615
(803) 234-0331

Anchor Floss
J.P. Coats Copper Metallic Thread

Westrim Crafts
9667 Canoga Avenue
Chatsworth, CA 91311
(800) 727-2727

3 x 6mm, 3mm, 2.5mm faux pearls

C. M. Offray and Son
360 Route 24
Chester, NJ 07930
(908) 879-4700

White Ribband 14

Willmaur Crafts
735 Old York Road
Willow Grove, PA 19090
(800) 523-2444

Cream Perforated Paper 14

Fairfield Processing Corp.
P.O. Box 1157
Danbury, CT 06813-1157
(800) 243-0989

Polyester stuffing
Fleece